JOHN PAUL II: THE PATH TO SAINTHOOD

Dedicated to the Staff at the Apostolic Palace, who shared
twenty six years of their lives with Blessed John Paul II.
With affection and respect.

MICHAEL COLLINS

John Paul II
The Path to
Sainthood

columba

First published in 2011 by
The Columba Press,
55A Spruce Avenue, Stillorgan Industrial Park,
Blackrock, Co Dublin

Designed by Bill Bolger
Photographs courtesy of Felici Brothers, Rome

Printed by Watermans, Cork

ISBN 978-185607-730-9

Contents

Pope John Paul blesses as he prepares to celebrate Mass in front of St Peter's Basilica

Preface

I first met Pope John Paul II in late June 1979. A friend and I had hitch-hiked from Dublin to Rome. We had both commenced studies for the priesthood the previous year. One morning, we received an invitation from the Pope's private secretary, Father John Magee, to meet the Pope. The pontiff was staying for a brief period in the Tower of St John in the Vatican gardens while his apartments were being renovated.

I recall how he walked into the room, exuding energy and cheerfulness. We were introduced to him along with other guests. After a short greeting, we had a photograph taken and then the Pope went out through the door, where a car was waiting to take him back to the Apostolic Palace for the day's meetings. I remember being startled as he slapped me on the shoulder as he left.

Fr Magee also sat into the car, and I looked out the door to signal my appreciation for his kindness in arranging the meeting. He discreetly nodded to me. The Pope, however, leaned forward and, with a broad smile on his face, gave me the "thumbs up" sign.

Over the next twenty five years, I met Pope John Paul on some thirty occasions. Several times in the early years I met him in the gardens of Castelgandolfo, when I spent my summers working as a guide in St Peter's Basilica. After ordination, I often concelebrated Mass either in his country residence or in the Vatican. He was always ready to chat. As a linguist, he enjoyed bantering in various languages.

Monsignor Thu, his Vietnamese secretary, told me that the Pope was deaf in one ear, which explained why he always turned to one side when talking with individuals.

I met Sr Tobiana on several occasions and was always deeply struck by her sincere love for the Pope and the care she showed him in his old age and illness. It was to her that he whispered his last words on earth and it was she who held his hand as he "slipped away to the House of the Lord."

As the years went by, the strong athletic man shrank in size, but he grew in my appreciation. His acceptance of physical illness and pain was extraordinary but his sheer determination was impressive. The last time I saw him was in the Papal Apartments one Sunday evening six months before he died. His face was now a mask, his body a like a crumpled blanket. Yet behind the pain-filled eyes was the soul of a man who burned with a deep love of Jesus Christ. He remains my inspiration and I realise that I am blessed to have met him.

Michael Collins

Introduction

As HE LAID HIS HEAD on the pillow in the early hours of 17 October 1978, Karol Wojtyla knew he would find little rest. Some nine hours earlier he had been elected 264th Pope, successor to the Apostle Peter, taking the name John Paul II.

The tumultuous hours which followed were but the presage of the changes which were about to engulf him. Emerging onto the balcony of St Peter's Basilica to give his blessing to the city and the world, Karol Wojtyla stepped into the blinding light of history.

The conclave which had elected him, with some 100 of the possible 111 votes, had ended shortly before 6.00 pm. Less than two months earlier, the same cardinals had elected Albino Luciani, the Patriarch of Venice, as Pope John Paul I. The smiling Venetian had quickly won the hearts of many, but his sudden death after thirty- three days in office had caused confusion and dismay.

The new Pope from Poland had asked the cardinals to remain with him until the next morning, when they would celebrate the first Mass of the new pontificate in the Sistine Chapel. After a genial meal, during which the cardinals sang him the traditional greeting Polish greeting *Sto lat* (May you live a hundred years) he had retired to his cell to outline a homily for the Mass.

The largest voting bloc had been the 55 Europeans, of which 25 were Italians. The sudden death of Pope John Paul I on 29 September had thrown many of the cardinals into panic. A new criterion was needed. The next Pope ought not to be too elderly, and certainly should be in good health. Nor indeed should he be too young. The old Italian saying applied – we want a Holy Father, not an Eternal Father

The front-runners were Cardinal Giovanni Benelli, Archbishop of Florence, and Cardinal Giuseppe Siri of Genoa. Benelli, a long-time Vatican diplomat, represented the moderately liberal cardinals. Siri had already given an interview to a newspaper, published on the eve of the conclave, announcing the conservative changes he would introduce if elected.

Each morning and afternoon, the cardinals cast their votes in two ballots. Dressed in scarlet robes, each stepped up one by one to the altar beneath Michaelangelo's towering fresco of the Last Judgement, calling on God to witness his vote. The folded ballot paper was placed on a silver paten dish, and then tipped into a chalice. After each vote, the ballots were tallied, and the names of the leading candidates called out.

After each ballot, the papers were burned in a stove. A chimney, leading from the chapel to the roof, was visible to the crowds gathered in St Peter's Square. Each unsuccessful ballot curled up in black smoke. The people drifted off into the surrounding bars to have a coffee and speculate on the proceedings inside the chapel. The papacy is the longest surviving non-hereditary monarchy in the world. Media networks mulled over the possible election of a new Pope and what it would mean to one billion Catholics and the world at large.

Many were critical of the medieval practice of electing the Pope, introduced almost a thousand years earlier. The exclusion of lay voices, of women, of a broad spectrum of experience, struck many as outmoded and unlikely to produce the best leader of the Catholic Church. For now, the conclave was the only way to elect a Pope, and the cardinals were intent on their work.

The cardinals themselves were also uncomfortable, with one hundred and eleven largely elderly men forced to live together for an indeterminate period. While many had complained in August of the sweltering temperatures, now they grumbled as the autumn drafts chilled their temporary accomodation. Fortunately modern conclaves were relatively short-lived affairs. The last lengthy conclave had lasted from 30 November 1799 to 14 March 1800, when Cardinal Giorgio Chiarmonti was elected Pius VII on the Island of San Giorgio in Venice. The longest conclave had been held in the town of Viterbo. Lasting 33 months between 1268-71, the cardinals finally settled on a candidate, Gregory X, when the mayor of the city had stripped the roof from the room in which they met and had reduced their food rations.

Only when white smoke unfurled into the dark Roman night sky would everyone know the conclave was over and a new Pope had been elected. The piazza would fill rapidly as news spread throughout the surrounding streets and people raced to hear the historic announcement.

Cardinal Benelli had come within less than a dozen votes of being elected. Both he and Cardinal Siri had gained rapidly and then abruptly lost their respective votes. The Italians were unable to decide on which candidate they wanted. With both frontrunners out of the papal race, the cardinals were now faced with the election of the first non-Italian Pope since the Dutch Adrian IV (1522-23).

Cardinal Franz Koenig of Vienna had suggested to the Primate of Poland, Cardinal Stefan Wyszynski that the time might be ripe for a Pope from Poland. The Primate modestly protested that Poland needed him, to which Koenig mildly replied that he had been thinking about Cardinal Karol Wojtyla. Cardinal Krol of Philadelphia, of Polish descent, and a number of other electors agreed with the candidate suggested by the Austrian cardinal. And so, on the second day of conclave, at the eighth ballot, Karol Wojtyla was elected to the papacy.

As he lay in bed, in the cell close to the Sistine Chapel, the new Pope's mind was teeming with memories of the past and plans for the future. His thoughts turned to his parents, his brother and sister Olga, the little girl he had had never even met. Did he imagine his fellow countrymen who flooded through the streets of Poland's cities and villages, cheering their compatriot? Would the path of his life until this moment prepare him to fulfill the dreams and hopes of so many?

The great themes of the pontificate about to unfold were born from his experiences in Poland and abroad. From the soil of Poland, immersed in the Catholic faith for a thousand years, Karol Wojtyla was the product of a rich history. As he had said to the people gathered in St Peter's Square earlier that evening, "the most eminent cardinals have called a new Bishop of Rome. They have called him from a far-away country... far, but always near in the communion of faith and the Christian tradition."

Who was Karol Wojtlya?

Karol Josef Wojtlya was born in the small town of Wadovice, some 50 kilometers from Krakow on 18 May, 1920. The town had about 10,000 inhabitants. He was the youngest of three children born to Karol Wotjyla, an army officer and Emilia Kaczorowska, a seamstress whose family originated in Lithuania.

The family circumstances were modest. Olga, the first of the children, had died in infancy, and Edmund, Karol's brother was 14 years his senior. The young boy was attached to his brother but Karol was forced to say farewell when Edmund decided to train as a doctor and left home to study medicine in Krakow.

Karol was sociable and enjoyed sports, especially football which he played in the local school grounds. Emilia was delicate and suffered with heart and lung problems for some years. These gradually grew more serious and when Karol was just 8 years of age, she died, at the age of 45. The loss of his mother made an enormous impact on him, and he continued to refer to her fondly throughout his life. Two years later, Edmund graduated as a doctor and came to work at Bielsko-Biala hospital, closer to Wadowice. Karol was able to see his brother on regular visits home. The two brothers grew much closer, united around their widowed father.

In November 1932, when Karol was just 12, another bitter tragedy occurred. Edmund became ill with scarlet fever, contracted in the hospital where he worked. Within a few days, on 4 December, he died in hospital. Speaking years later to his friend Andre Frossard, John Paul confided how grievously he felt the bereavement.

"My mother's death made a deep impression on me. My brother's perhaps a still deeper one because of the dramatic circumstances in which it occurred and because I was more mature. Thus quite soon I became a motherless only child"

Karol senior tried his best to look after his remaining child. While the days were filled with school lessons, serving Mass, playing football, the evenings were passed at home with his father. Often the two made a pilgrimage to a shrine at Kalwaria Zebrzydowska. The sanctuary, dedicated to the Passion of Christ, was established in 1600 and consists of 42 chapels. Here Passion plays were performed in Holy Week. At home, father and son recited the Rosary and prayers together, and, before bed, Karol senior told patriotic stories of Poland's tortured past.

At the age of 18, Karol graduated from Wadowice School and decided to enrol at the Jagiellonian University in Krakow. His studies were in Polish literature and history. Leaving their rented apartment in Church Street, the two Wojtylas travelled to Krakow in order for Karol to be near the university. They took up lodgings in the basement flat at 10, Tyniecka Street, a house owned by Emelia's brother, Robert Kaczorowski.

By now Karol senior was 60, and had retired on a small military pension. While the young Karol enthusiastically embraced student life, his father cared for the house and cooked meals. Karol quickly made friends at university and soon was drawn into a circle of amateur actors, Studio 39, who performed largely patriotic plays and recitals of poetry. He later joined the Rhapsodic Theatre, an underground theatrical movement, which allowed him foster his love of acting.

At the beginning of his second year at university, life was to change dramatically once more for Karol. On 1 September, Germany invaded Poland. The Second World War had begun and for the next six years, the country was to be engulfed in one of the most horrific wars in human history.

Along with hundreds of citizens of Krakow, both father and son left the city at the beginning of the hostilities. When they reached the River San, some 120 miles east of Krakow, they learned that Russia had invaded Poland. Faced with the onslaught from Russia, the two returned to Krakow. The Nazi troops were deemed less hostile than the fierce Russians.

With the university closed, Karol was forced to work in a quarry. A work permit was required by the authorities. Lack of such a permit could result in deportation to a concentration camp. The young man began work on 11 October 1940. Each day Karol travelled outside the city to the quarry at Zakrzówek, where he was detailed to the explosives unit. The work at the quarry and later at a chemical plant allowed him the necessary permit to avoid deportation. On a return trip home as Pope, he met his former colleagues, and recalled the kindness of the supervisor, who allowed him read his university books.

In late 1941, Karol's father became ill. Forced to remain in bed, his health continued to deteriorate. Karol divided his time between lectures and caring for his father. Returning home one afternoon in mid February 1942, Karol discovered that his father had collapsed and died in his bedroom, apparently from a heart attack. At the age of 20, Karol was now entirely alone. Having called the priest, he spent the whole night praying beside his father.

For six months he went to stay with the family of his friend Juliusz Kydrynski and he was transferred to the Solvay chemical plant. The loss of his father had forced him to re-evaluate his life. The war had disrupted his studies, and once more he determined a change of course. He decided to become a priest. Influenced by Jan Leopold Tyranowski, who ran the Living Rosary Group in St. Stanislaw Kosta Parish, Karol was torn between joining the Carmelites or the diocese of Krakow. He enrolled in the Sodality of Our Lady of Mount Carmel, and received the brown scapular.

Having taken advice from the local curate in his parish, Karol finally decided to become a priest in Krakow diocese. He went to visit Cardinal Adam Sapieha, who recalled how the young Karol had given a welcome address many years earlier when the cardinal had visited his school. The cardinal was impressed by the serious young man, but explained clearly the danger which his training would involve. The Nazis had closed the seminary, so classes were held clandestinely. Karol attended lectures when his shift work allowed. Seminary training also meant that he had to leave the Rhapsodic Theatre, much to the disappointment of his fellow actors.

On 29 February, while walking home from the factory, Karol was hit by a German truck. Left unconscious for some hours, he was transferred to hospital where he remained for twelve days. When in August the Nazis held searches in the neighbourhood for seminarians, the archbishop decided it was safer for them to live in the episcopal residence. Karol joined the other nine seminarians and concluded his studies under the tutelage of the archbishop, whom he came to know and respect. On 18 January 1945, the Russian Army ousted the Nazis from Krakow, but the sufferings of the city were not yet over.

A year after the war ended, Karol was ordained by Cardinal Sapieha in the private chapel of the palace on 1 November 1946. He was the first of his class to be ordained. The next day, the Commemoration of the Faithful Departed, Fr Wojtyla cele-

Karoj Wojtyla was
Poland's youngest
bishop and later, the
country's youngest
cardinal.

Karoj Wojtyla was Poland's youngest bishop and later, the country's youngest cardinal.

brated his first Mass in the crypt of the medieval Wawel
Cathedral, in the heart of Krakow. A fortnight later, on 15
November, he boarded a train bound for Rome. The cardinal
had decided that the newly ordained priest was capable of further studies and sent him to study at the Dominican university
of the Angelicum.

The exposure to Rome gave the young Fr Wojtlya an invaluable
lesson in the universality of the Church. While lodging in the
Belgian College, he learned French and his daily contacts
allowed him learn Italian. He immediately took to the city,

spending his free time visiting the churches and, in particular, the catacombs. He also assisted in parish work when his studies permitted. During his summer vacations, he travelled throughout France, improving his knowledge of French while learning about developments in the post-war Church.

Over the next two years, he worked on a thesis on St John of the Cross, graduating with highest marks. On 15 June 1948, the day after he received his doctorate, the young priest returned to Poland, where he was appointed as curate to the village of Niegowici. The Poland to which he returned was markedly different from that which he had left. Communists were in power, and relations between Church and State had soured. The young priest enjoyed his first parish, remarking to a friend that the farmers whom he met were wiser than the Greek philosophers. Years later, villagers remembered the earnest young priest who walked around the district in a black soutane and biretta, stopping to exchange a few words with everybody he met. He was conscientious and in particular-spent a long time with penitents who came to celebrate the Sacrament of Penance.

It was during this time that he began to write for a Catholic newspaper based in Krakow, *Tygodnik Powszechny*. His first article was on his observations of the Church in France which he had visited during his study leave. For years he would remain a faithful associate journalist, publishing poetry and essays on religious and ethical topics.

The experience in the rural parish was short-lived, and less than a year later he was transferred to the urban setting of St Florian's Parish in Krakow. The university was nearby and many students and academics frequented the church. The young Fr Karol made friends easily and became very popular. He was in great demand for marriages and baptisms, and ran regular retreats for engaged couples. It was unusual to have such a highly qualified curate, but he made his mark felt with those who frequented the university.

Shortly before he died, Cardinal Sapieha decided that the academic young priest should do another doctorate, this time in philosophy. Although he continued to reside in a parochial house, he undertook a two- year doctorate on the German philosopher Max Scheler. Contemporaries recalled the young Fr Wojtyla as quiet and reserved, but passionate once he was engaged in debate.

Relations between the Church and the Communist government continued to deteriorate. In late 1952, police arrested Monsignor Eugeniusz Baziak, the Archbishop of Krakow, and a year later, the Primate of Poland, Cardinal Wyszynski of Warsaw was imprisoned for thirty-five months. When President Wladyslaw Gomulka was elected President of Poland in 1953, Cardinal Wyszynski was released, to the delight of the Catholics and the resentment of the Communists.

Plans for Fr Wojtyla to teach on the Theology Faculty at the Jagellonian University in Krakow were abandoned when the faculty was abolished in 1953. But a university post awaited him. In 1954, he began to lecture on Social Ethics at the Catholic University of Lublin University and was appointed to the Chair of Ethics two years later.

While he continued his chaplaincy work in Krakow, the young professor travelled every fortnight to Lublin where he gave lectures. In order to save time, he took the overnight train, arriving in Lublin with barely enough time to fulfill the obligations of his lecture timetable. However, Professor Wojtyla was very popular with his students, many of whom would accompany him back to the train station for his return to Krakow.

On 4 July 1958, while on a canoeing holiday in the mountains, Karol Wojtyla received a telephone call to visit Cardinal Wyszynski in Warsaw. An auxiliary had died, and Pope Pius XII had appointed the young academic as the new auxiliary of Krakow. It was one of Pope Pius' last appointments, as he died in October of that year.

WHO WAS KAROL VOJTLYA?

When Fr Wojtlya protested to the archbishop that thirty-eight was too young to be consecrated a bishop, the prelate dryly remarked that God would soon relieve him of that impediment.

Accepting the appointment, the new auxiliary surprised the archbishop by asking for permission to return to his vacation with his students and friends in the mountains. He had been preparing a book on sexual ethics, and he had distributed several chapters to his companions. The Primate, who did not know the bishop elect, gave permission to the unusual request, urging him to be back in time for his consecration. He had not yet learned the young cleric's unpunctuality. Fr Wojtyla went to the nearby convent of Ursuline nuns. Knocking on the door, he asked if he could pray in the chapel. He remained for such a long time in prayer that a sister came to see if he was well. She was surprised to find him prostrate on the floor before the tabernacle. It was a mode of prayer he continued to use into old age.

The date was set for his episcopal consecration. On 28 September, Karol Wojtyla was consecrated at Wawel Cathedral and immediately took up his new duties. He was the youngest bishop in Poland.

Bishop Wojtyla was plunged into the world of Polish politics. Hitherto he had shown no interest in the Communist regime. Now, as pastor, he had to deal with the authorities who actively interfered with the life of the Church.

One of his first encounters with the antagonistic atheistic Communist authorities concerned the industrial town of Nowa Huta. Built in the suburbs of Krakow, the city planners refused permission to build a church. Each year, usually on Christmas Eve, Bishop Wojtyla celebrated Mass in the open air. It was an effective move, subtly putting the authorities under pressure and making their refusal look ridiculous in public opinion. Finally, in 1967, they relented and permission was granted to build the parish church. For over a decade, workers and students came from all over Poland to offer their services for free. The church was dedicated by Cardinal Wojtyla the year before his election to the papacy. A stone from St Peter's tomb, sent by Pope Paul VI, was placed in the church.

Bishop Wojtyla retained his academic interest, lecturing to students and in 1960 publishing his first book, *Love and Responsibility*. He also began to cooperate with Cardinal Wyszynski's great novena, a nine year period of preparation for the millennium of Polish Christianity celebrated in 1966.

When Archbishop Baziak died in July 1962, the auxiliary was elected as a stopgap administrator. Pope John XXIII had convoked the Second Vatican Council which was due to open on 11 October that same year. Bishop Wojtyla had submitted a paper to the Preparatory Commission in 1959 outlining the need for a new presentation of Christian humanism. In particular, he urged a review of the way in which lay people were seen as a passive force. Bishop Wojtyla departed for Rome on 5 October and participated in the first sessions, held between October and December.

The visit to Rome enkindled old memories of his student days, but importantly introduced him to many of the world's leading theologians. He found the sessions themselves somewhat boring, but he enjoyed the informal gatherings and also broadened his knowledge of the universal Church. Seated far away from the High Altar, close to the main door, Bishop Wojtlya spent the tedious sessions composing poetry and preparing the outline of a book. Returning to Krakow, he wrote many articles about the Council and initiated a series of visits to the parishes of the diocese. In particular, he tried to interest the priests in the changes which were about to sweep the Church.

On 3 June 1963, Pope John XXIII died at the Vatican. For two years the Pope had suffered from stomach cancer, and with his death, the Church lost one of its best-loved Popes. The Archbishop of Milan, Giovanni Battista Montini was elected as Paul VI. The new Pope would play an important part in the life of Karol Wojtlya. In the autumn, he returned to Rome for the second session of the Council, held once more between October and December and took part in a pilgrimage made by the Council Fathers to the Holy Land. As the year ended, surprising news came from Rome. For eighteen months the Vatican and Communist authorities had been negotiating on the position of the new Archbishop of Krakow. Karol Wojtyla was appointed to the See on 30 December. He was just 43.

The installation took place on 8 March at Wawel Cathedral, where seven years earlier he had been consecrated the youngest bishop in Poland. He was now the second senior prelate in Poland, after Cardinal Wyszynski of Warsaw. With his new post came an apartment in the Archbishop's Palace, but he chose to remain in his old lodgings in Via Kanonicza.

Returning to Rome in September for the third session of the Council, Archbishop Wojtyla was now deeply immersed in the broadening work of the Council. He made several contributions from the floor, and was the only bishop to greet the women present at the sessions in his opening address. When the session ended on 21 November, he left for a two-week pilgrimage in the Holy Land. The Council was due to close the following year. It was time to produce the final documents. In the Holy Land he worked on ideas for the great decree *Gaudium et Spes*, the optimistic document on the Church in the contemporary world. During the Spring of 1965, he visited Rome several times to work on the document with other theologians and bishops. As Pope, John Paul would regularly quote from the decree on which he had so closely worked and to which he had contributed.

When the Council closed on 8 December, Karol Wojtyla returned to Poland and threw himself into the Great Millennium celebrations which began on 1 January 1966. The year was full of mass gatherings and pilgrimages. Cardinal Wyszynski's strategy worked. Millions of Poles participated in the liturgies, processions and events which greatly irritated the Communist authorities. The highlight was a Solemn Mass at the shrine of the Black Madonna at Czestochowa. Pope Paul VI had been invited by the hierarchy, but the Communist government made it impossible for the pontiff to come to Poland.

The following year, on 28 June, Karol Wojtyla was created a cardinal in the Sistine Chapel. It was a sign of Pope Paul VI's approval of the Polish prelate whom he admired. When Pope Paul set up a commission to study the regulation of birth control, he appointed Wojtyla as a member. Although he did not attend the Roman meetings, he finally voted in favour of maintaining the Church's traditional teaching on contraception.

In the year of his appointment, the UB (the Polish secret police) circulated an internal memo on the new cardinal's qualities: "It can be said that Wojtyla is one of the few intellectuals in the Polish Episcopate. He deftly reconciles...traditional

Pope Paul VI receives the newly-created Cardinal Wojtyla at an audience in the Vatican

WHO WAS KAROL VOJTLYA?

popular religiosity with intellectual Catholicism...he has not, so far, engaged in open anti-state activity. It seems that politics are his weaker suit; he is over-intellectualized...He lacks organizing and leadership qualities, and this is his weakness..."

The authorities soon changed their opinion, and for the remaining years in Krakow the archbishop's rooms were bugged with listening devices. The archbishop was aware, and often took guests outside to the garden to talk where he believed he would not be overheard. In his dealings with the Communist authorities, he became increasingly astute, and was regarded as a formidable foe.

On 10 January, the cardinal finally agreed to move into the large apartments traditionally used by the Archbishop of Krakow on Via Franciskanska. Rather than use the large ornate bedroom, he slept in a small side bedroom. The elaborate study was rarely used, as Archbishop Wojtyla preferred to sit at his wooden desk at the back of his private chapel, praying, writing and reading. Each Friday morning he crossed the road to the Franciscan Church where he prayed the Stations of the Cross.

The cardinal began to use his increased profile to challenge the Communist authorities. He continued to visit new parishes, and during homilies he was critical of the way in which Poland had developed. During 1968, Cardinal Wojtyla made 122 visits to the parishes of the archdiocese of Krakow, accompanying the image of the Black Madonna. He also re-vitalised the *Corpus Christi* Processions, hitherto prohibited by the Communists. During these ceremonies, Cardinal Wojtyla's rhetoric improved, as he used his ringing baritone voice and stirred up the imagination of his listeners. He also was attentive to the needs of his priests. He urged them at all times to avoid ostentation and live more frugal lives, dedicated to prayer and the pastoral care of the people in the diocese.

When Cardinal Wyszynski was refused a passport by the Communist authorities to travel to Rome for the first Synod of

Bishops in 1972, Cardinal Wojtyla also refused to travel as a sign of solidarity for the Primate. Such prohibitions, however, were to backfire on the Communist government, which was shown to be petty and opposed to freedom of movement. Cardinal Wyszynski complained bitterly that the Holy See did not understand the depth of sufferings Polish Catholic enduring under the increasingly hostile Communist government.

The cardinal was inspired by the idea of the Synod of Bishops in Rome and replicated the concept in Krakow. In 1972, he inaugurated a seven-year synod which had not fully concluded by the time he was elected to the papacy in 1978.

In 1973, Cardinal Wojtyla decided to visit the Polish diaspora, travelling to Australia, New Guinea, the Philippines, Belgium and France. Further plans to travel had to be postponed the following year when he was appointed the principal relator of the Synod of Bishops on Evangelisation. The Holy Year of 1975, brought him to Rome for pilgrimages and a number of ceremonies, but foreign travel resumed again in 1976 when he made a six-week visit to the Polish communities in the United States. That same year he received a special mark of favour from Pope Paul VI, when he was asked to preach the Spiritual Exercises for the Pope and his Curia during Lent. The five-day retreat exposed the Polish prelate to a number of influential cardinals at the Vatican. While noting Wojtyla's piety, they observed how well at ease he was and the authority with which he spoke.

By now, many of the young people who had listened to the young professor were married, and had children and grandchildren. Even as a cardinal, Karol Wojtyla continued to join his friends on country excursions, and enjoy canoeing along the rivers and lakes of his beloved Tatra mountains.

These were thus the formative years for the papacy. All the events which were to gain the attention of the world were already in place in the life of Karol Wojtyla, now John Paul II.

Pope John Paul was the most demonstrative pontiff in modern times.

JOHN PAUL II: THE PATH TO SAINTHOOD

Daily Life with John Paul

The day after his election as Pope, John Paul II was accompanied by the Camerlengo, Cardinal Villot, to the Papal Apartments. The doors of the apartment had been sealed with red ribbon and wax after the sudden death of his predecessor on 29 September. These rooms would become his home for the next quarter of a century, and here he was to die on 2 April 2005.

The Apostolic Palace was built by the great Renaissance architect Domenico Fontana for Pope Sixtus V (1585-90). Throughout the 17th and 18th centuries, the Popes resided in the Quirinal Palace, on the Quirinal Hill in the heart of Rome. When Rome became the capital of a united Italy in July 1871, Pope Pius IX (1846-78) abandoned the Quirinal and took up residence in the large square building overlooking St Peter's Square.

Although nominally the whole palace served as the official papal residence, Pope Pius X (1903-14) found the rooms too large. He came from poor farming stock in the north east of Italy. He was deeply uncomfortable amid the trappings of the aristocratic papacy. Immediately following his election, he withdrew to the upper floor, where seven rooms were laid out for him. Subsequent Popes retained the small area. Pius XII (1939-58) lived in a separate area close to St Peter's during the Second World War, while Pope Paul VI (1963-78) had the whole apartments redecorated in neutral pastel colours. It was to this apartment that Pope John Paul moved after his election.

Visitors enter the Papal Apartments from the *loggia*, or corridor decorated by the school of Raphael in the 16th century. A Swiss Guard stands outside the rectangular oak doors. One enters a small antechamber before the apartments open into a large rectangular room.

The room has three windows on the side which open on to St Peter's Square. From the room opens a corridor off which are the priest secretary's office, the Pope's study and the pontiff's bedroom. Each room is also interconnected by doors. These last three rooms can be seen from the Square on the upper right hand. The Pope's bedroom has three windows, one opening to the Square, the other two towards Castelsantangelo. The room was divided by a screen and a desk was placed in the corner where the Pope could continue working.

Each morning, the Pope rose at 5.00 am. After showering and dressing, he crossed the corridor from his bedroom to the small chapel where he began the day with prayer. These early hours were vitally important for him. As he knelt on the bronze pre-dieu before the altar, he spoke to God about his hopes, expressed his worries and confided his cares. Underneath the small kneeler, one of the Sisters placed letters from all around the world, requests from the faithful for prayers and remembrance at Mass.

After about an hour, he rose, genuflected to the Blessed Sacrament in the tabernacle, and went behind the altar, where vestments were laid out in a small sacristy. Over the vesting table was a large crucifix, flanked by porcelain statues of the Blessed Virgin Mary and St John.

Once vested, he returned to his pre-dieu, and continued his prayers. The chapel, decorated with a white marble and porphyry revetment and stained glass windows by Marc Chagall, was renovated for Pope Paul VI during the early 1970's. A large bronze crucifix hung over the altar and to the side an image of Our Lady of Czestochowa. Traditionally the Pope celebrated Mass with his two priest secretaries and household staff. John Paul invariably invited guests each morning. Some were friends from Poland or Rome, and often bishops on *ad limina*, their five yearly visits to the Holy See. The guests would number between twenty and thirty. The Pope celebrated Mass towards the crucifix, rather than the more common table altar in parish churches.

When Mass was finished, the guests filed out and waited for ten or fifteen minutes until the Pope had concluded his thanksgiving prayers in the chapel. As he came into the corridor, he greeted the guests, giving each a rosary as a memento of their visit. By 8.00 am, he bade farewell to his guests and went into the adjacent dining room where he took his small breakfast of orange juice, coffee, bread and pastries. Occasionally when

DAILY LIFE WITH JOHN PAUL

time permitted, guests were also invited to the brief breakfast. Shortly after 8.30 am, the Pope was normally at his desk in his small study. To his right the window opened onto St Peter's Square. In the early morning he could hear the water from the fountain below. Behind him were bookshelves as well as small souvenirs which friends and visitors had given him. On the long shelf behind his chair he kept family photographs. The Pope showed little interest in his surroundings. When work-men were finally allowed in to renovate the apartments follow-ing the election of Pope Benedict XVI, the electricity was found to be unsafe and the heating system quite inadequate to warm the Pope's home.

The personnel in the private apartments was small. Five Polish nuns, Handmaids of the Sacred Heart, looked after his needs. Sr Tobiana Sobodka was a medical nurse by training and cared for him during his illnesses. Sr Germana looked after the kitchen, preparing Polish and Italian food. St Fernanda was in charge of provisions, while Sr Matylda cared for the wardrobe and vestments used by the Pope. Sr Eufrosyna attended to the Pope's private correspondence, and in later years the Pope dic-tated all his work to her. The Pope's valet, Angelo Gugel, who entered service in 1978, looked after all the pontiff's needs. He prepared the dining room for meals and served them, as well as caring for the Pope's wardrobe. Originally from the Veneto region of Northern Italy, Gugel also accompanied the pontiff on each occasion he left the apartments for audiences, both within the Vatican and on papal visits. In his old age, the fragile and infirm pontiff was dressed by his faithful valet.

The Pope had regular medical check- ups with his physician, Renato Buzzonetti. Although Buzzonetti was almost always in service, three other doctors took turns to attend the Pope when the need arose.

Throughout his pontificate, Pope John Paul retained his pri-vate secretary, Stanislaw Dziwisz. A priest of the diocese of Krakow, Dziwisz had become the archbishop's secretary in

1966 and was to remain with his mentor until his death thirty-nine years later.

The role of secretary is full-time and demanding, literally seven days a week. The Popes retained two priest secretaries. Pope Paul had asked an Irish Missionary of St Patrick, Father John Magee, to assist him during the Holy Year of 1975 and he stayed with Pope Paul until his death on 6 August 1978. The Irishman was then assumed by Pope John Paul I and assisted the pontiff during his month-long papacy. While collecting his personal belongings shortly after the election of Pope John Paul, the Polish Pope greeted him with a warm embrace. He asked the Irish priest to remain and assist him. Here he remained until 1984 when he was appointed Master of Liturgical Celebrations.

The Pope chose an African priest from the Democratic Republic of the Congo, Emery Kabungo to succeed him and after three years, a Vietnamese priest, Vincent Thu replaced him. The diminutive secretary, who was three years older than the Pope, remained in his service until 1996, when the last secretary, Mieczyslaw Mokrzycki, was appointed.

Between 8.30 and 9.00 am, the private secretary gave him briefings and a précis with updates on the world situation. Phone calls were pencilled into the diary for different times of the day, according to global time zones. By 9.00 am, the secretary left him to work on his own. Often he crossed the corridor where he sat at a little desk as in his days at Krakow. Drafts of homilies, encyclicals and other religious documents were usually born in the chapel. Monsignor Thu recalled how unassuming the Pope was with his staff. "He always came into our office if he needed pencils or paper. If anything was lacking, he made no fuss. And he never retired for the evening without visiting the Sisters and thanking them for their service that day."

The Pope never learned how to type. He often joked at how many "ghost-writers," he had at his disposal. He wrote the

Watched over by his secretary of 39 years, Stanislaw Dziwisz, Pope John Paul signs a book.

main ideas in Polish, and short indications in Latin. These were then circulated around the various offices in the Vatican. When he composed encyclicals, he took on one or two assistants to whom he gave the work of putting his thematic thoughts into prose.

At 11.00 am, the Prefect of the Papal Household arrived to accompany the Pope to the floor below where audiences were held in the Apostolic Library. Most visits, usually of heads of state, or politicians, were finished within 20 minutes, although as the Pope became older these were cut to a bare minimum.

Lunch was served around 1.30 pm, often in the company of the last guests to have met the pontiff. The food was normally Italian, while Polish food was served on Sundays and feast days. On Sundays, the Pope liked especially to have Polish-speaking friends, most notably Cardinal Andrej Deskur, who regaled the company with jokes he had picked up during the week. Pope John Paul once remarked that he wished he could appoint him as Jester to the Papal Court.

After lunch, the Pope took a walk on his own along the open air roof-top terrace above the Apostolic Palace. The square-shaped building is set around a courtyard five stories high, and the terrace runs along the four inner sides. The terrace, divided by a series of walls, is decorated with potted orange and lemon trees as well as palm trees and other large plants. On the inside the square opens onto the dark internal courtyard. On the exterior, the terrace gives on to spectacular view of Rome, of the Janiculum Hill and far beyond to the Sabine Hills.

For a man who loved the open air and nature, the confines of the Vatican were often stifling, and on one occasion he ruefully referred to the Vatican as "a gilded cage". Returning to his desk shortly after 3.30, the Pope worked until 6.00 p.m when he began the evening audiences. These were normally with the Secretary of State, Cardinal Joseph Ratzinger or Cardinal Re, or other cardinals, according to the day. He also frequently met with his Press Officer, the Spaniard Joaquin Navarro-Valls,

Even as Pope, Karol Wojtyla loved to escape to the mountains where he skiied and walked.

when issues needed to be responded to in the media. These routine meetings ended at 7.30, allowing the Pope half an hour to pray Vespers in the Chapel before supper at 8.00.

The light supper, to which guests were sometimes invited, ended about 8.45. As in many Italians homes, a television was placed in the corner of the dining room. Occasionally the Pope and his staff watched the News or a programme of interest.

The day's work was not yet done. A dossier, prepared by the Secretariate of State, was placed on his desk and the pontiff spent an hour or so working before retiring to his bedroom where he read. Each evening before he went to bed, he stood behind the curtains in his room, gazing out onto the city, which he blessed. His last reading was reserved for the lives of the Saints which greatly inspired him.

JOHN PAUL II: THE PATH TO SAINTHOOD

From the terrace of the pontifical villa at Castelgandolfo, the newly-elected Pope John Paul looks out on Lake Albano

During the summer and for a week after Christmas and Easter, the Pope went to the papal residence at Castelgandolfo, some 20 km outside Rome. The rhythm of daily life varied little from that in the Vatican. Shortly after he was elected, Polish Americans gave him a gift of funds to build a swimming pool. When the Pope was criticised for accepting the donation, he quipped, "it is cheaper than another conclave."

Karol Wojtyla loved to escape to the mountains, and on several occasions, he slipped from Castelgandolfo to the hills at nearby Ovindoli. Until he fractured his hip in his early 70's the Pope would go skiing. The Communist President of Italy, Sandro Pertini, once joined him in 1984 on the slopes at Adamello and the two struck up a strong friendship. His private secretary, Stanislaw Dziwisz, recorded that the Pope made about one hundred such escapades. The first time he left was in January 1981. Seated in the back of the car of Father Josef Kowalczy, another Polish priest Tadeusz Rakoczy held a newspaper open, so as to shield the Pope from prying eyes

Dressed in a navy ski suit, woolen cap and sunglasses, he joined the queues like any other skier, with one of the priests ahead and behind him. A ski-pass which had been purchased for him allowed him take the snow cars up the hill. Only on one occasion was he recognised by a young boy. However, the child was chased away by one of the priests accompanying the Pope before he could alert the bystanders.

During the summer, he often left the Vatican on Tuesdays with no guard in order to walk for a few hours in the forests. In his late '70s, the Pope began to vacation for two weeks in Val D'Aosta, or other parts of Northern Italy. Here he could enjoy fresh air, his beloved mountains and a proper break from the gruelling schedule which made up the daily life of the Pope.

The Pope Governs the Curia

"I am going to have lunch with the Pope"

Behind this innocuous remark there were layers of meaning. It often was a coded message for circumventing the tortuous protocol governing access to the Pope. For centuries, the Curia ran the Vatican. An Italian saying runs: "The Pope governs, the Curia rules."

The Pope, as Bishop of Rome and successor to St Peter, enjoys a unique position within the Church. Although in the past there were many despotic Popes, the modern papacy seeks to act as a focus of unity for both Catholics and all Christians. The Curia, in its present format, dates largely from the 16th century while the most recent reform was carried out in 1967 by Pope Paul VI, himself a former Vatican diplomat.

Various offices, called Congregations, oversee the Church's doctrine, moral life, episcopate, clergy and religious life. While one office cares for mission territories, others are dedicated to evangelising lands once historically Christian.

Within weeks of his election, the new Pope began to visit workers in their offices. Little did they imagine that in the coming years their workload would increase dramatically. Although the Vatican is at the heart of the Church which numbers more than 1.1 billion Catholics, the administration is comparatively slow.

Six months after the beginning of the pontificate, the Secretary of State the French Cardinal Jean Villot died. John Paul chose Agostino Casaroli, an experienced diplomat who had worked assiduously to improve conditions between Church and State in Eastern Europe. Observers were surprised at the choice. Casaroli had been part of the *Ostpolitik*. This Vatican strategy was based on the belief that the Communists were a stable force in Eastern Europe and compromise had to be reached with them. Wojtyla did not share this view and always believed Communism would collapse. However, until his retirement in December 1990 Casaroli collaborated with the Pope on a daily basis.

Pope John Paul did not hide his unhappiness with the ponderous rhythms of the various offices. He resolved to introduce a new reform. In 1984 , he appointed Cardinal Sebastian Baggio to oversee the gargantuan task. With the pontiff's goading, the reform was put into effect with the publication of the Apostolic Constitution *Pastor Bonus* four years later in June 1988. In effect, the result was a draw between Pope and the Curia. Almost entirely staffed by Italians for some four centuries, the Curia was akin to a civil service. Popes generally did not have extraordinarily long pontificates, and the government survived them. Pope John Paul II was out of the Vatican for 881 days of his pontificate on various pastoral trips. This block of two and a half years could be doubled by the amount of time spent on preparing for the visits and on recovery.

But Pope John Paul was too accessible for the comfort of some in the Curia who argued that the piazza or corridor was not the place to do business. It was not unusual for an official to receive a memo from the Pope inquiring about a particular sit-

Joseph Ratzinger was Pope John Paul's chief theological advisor for 25 years.

uation which had not been dealt with satisfactorily. The Pope's source was usually somebody unknown who had not gone through the proper channels. A guest at dinner or somebody he met during an audience. Occasionally a visitor from Krakow would murmur, "he was just like that in Poland."

As he grew older and more infirm, John Paul's declining health robbed him of his stamina. He relied increasingly on his secretaries, particularly Don Stanislaw, who became the virtual doorkeeper. A "kitchen cabinet" was formed, consisting of the Secretary of State and his Substitute as well as Cardinal Joseph Ratzinger. For the last two years of his life, these prelates were effectively governing the Church. Since 1982, Cardinal Ratzinger was Prefect of the Congregation for the Doctrine of the Church and as such was the pontiff's prime theological advisor. He suggested many of the ghost writers of the Pope's 14 encyclicals, and reviewed each before publication.

Another method of broadening the scope of the Curia was to appoint cardinals from around the globe. While Pope Paul VI had set the number of cardinal electors (those under 80) at 120, Pope John Paul II superseded the limit on two occasions.

THE POPE GOVERNS THE CURIA

Several of these were subsequently summoned to Rome and appointed as heads of various offices. The number of Italians decreased while there was an increase in the number of Poles and other Eastern Europeans employed as the pontiffs "eyes and ears."

Yet the Pope also managed to encourage the Curia, occasionally charming them or cajoling them into cooperation. He had a small but gifted corps of assistants, and he delegated to them according to the talents available.

When he was elected, Cardinal Wyszynski told Karol Wojtyla that it would be his task to lead the Church across the threshold into the new Millennium. In 1996, Pope John Paul began to plan for the Millennium, designating a three-year period of preparation. It was reminiscent of the nine-year novena in preparation for the Millennium celebrations of Polish Christianity which had concluded in 1966. He mobilised the cardinals and Curia and during the year, despite serious health problems, presided over a number of Jubilee events. The Polish Jubilee had strengthened the national Church. He hoped the Jubilee of the year 2000 would fortify the universal Church.

John Paul had learned how to govern and he delegated to his team of fellow workers. The Code of Canon Law, published in 1983, was an effort to unify the Church following the turbulent years after the Second Vatican Council. The Synod of Bishops, which had become a feature of Church life since the 1970's, gave the bishops of the world the opportunity of meeting regularly and of sharing experiences. The Pope presided over 15 synods and used the meetings to improve the dialogue between the Holy See and the bishops throughout the globe.

The Catechism of the Catholic Church was one of the pontificate's highpoints. The Compendium of Catholic Teaching was the first official compendium produced since the Council of Trent in the 16th century.

John Paul, Parish Priest of the World

Speaking to reporters during a press conference some days after his election, the Polish pontiff remarked:

"The Pope cannot remain a prisoner of the Vatican. I want to go to everybody...from the nomads of the steppes to the monks and nuns in their convents...I want to cross the threshold of every home."

During the 26 years of his pontificate, John Paul was to become the most widely-travelled Pope in history and the person seen by most people on the planet. He visited 129 countries during 104 papal trips outside Italy, logging up more than 750,000 miles. This corresponded to 30 times around the globe or three times the distance to the moon. By the end of his pontificate, only China and Russia were closed to him, due to the refusal of their respective governments to issue formal invitations.

Following the Millennium celebrations in Poland in 1966, Archbishop Wojtyla increasingly made international contacts. After his elevation to the College of Cardinals in 1967, he

On his first visit to Poland in June 1979, the Pope returned to his adoptive city of Krakow

broadened his circle of acquaintances. Most visits outside Poland were to Rome or countries where there was a large Polish population.

Pope Paul VI (1963-78) was the first modern pontiff to undertake pastoral journeys, visiting Jordan, Israel, Lebanon, India, the United States of America, Portugal, Turkey, Colombia, Bermuda, Switzerland, Uganda, Iran, Pakistan, the Philippines, Samoa, Australia, Hong Kong and Ceylon. Pope John Paul built on the achievements of his predecessor, visiting almost every country which had invited him.

The cost of the pastoral visits was met by the Catholic population and by the government which had extended the invitation. Security was an enormous drain, and several assassination attempts were foiled.

The Pope threw himself into the trips with gusto. Although he spoke eight languages, he learned to speak in several others, such as Japanese and Korean, phonetically. During a visit to Japan, the television commentators, used to translating the speeches of visiting dignitaries, stopped speaking and allowed the viewers listen to the Pope address them in their own

The Pope greets well-wishers from the window of his former home on Via Franciskanska

language. When he was told shortly after his election that almost half the world spoke Spanish, he replied, "It is time I joined that half.'

Immediately following his election, Pope John Paul received an invitation to open the CELAM conference in Mexico, a meeting of the bishops of Latin America. Although his predecessor had declined to attend, John Paul II enthusiastically embraced it. The visit to the Americas captured his imagination. There was a Marian shrine, the population was Catholic and the Mexican government, the anti-religious Industrial Revolutionary Party, needed to be challenged. The Pope made the first of his five visits to Mexico in January 1979. The Church was oppressed by the Government, and John Paul's visit highlighted the discrimination against Catholics, which make up the largest religion of the country.

Plans to visit the United States were extended to include a pastoral visit to Ireland. At Dublin's Phoenix Park, he celebrated Mass with a congregation of some one and a quarter million worshippers. The first visit to the United States brought him into contact with strands within and without the Church calling for change, in particular regarding the admission of women to the priesthood and ethical issues.

The Pope greets a young girl shortly after his election

Several countries drew him back repeatedly. Poland, so much in his blood, proved an irresistible attraction and on nine occasions he returned to his homeland. Three million gathered as he celebrated Mass in Victory Square in Warsaw in 1979. Welcomed as a hero at his first visit to Poland, by his last visit in 2002, the political situation had changed dramatically, and so had Polish society. As an old man, he railed against what he saw as the wrong direction many of his compatriots had taken when Communism collapsed.

He had a deep concern for France and visited the country on eight occasions. He made seven visits to the United States, including two stop- overs in Alaska. He visited Brazil on four occasions in an effort to stem the large number of Catholics who were joining Pentecostalist Churches.

He enjoyed the trips enormously, even if they exhausted him. Cardinal Roberto Tucci, who was the planner of the papal trips for many years, recorded how the easy the Pope was to organise. "He never asked where he was to stay, what the food would be like, what the temperature would be during the trip." On one occasion, returning from a trip to Latin America, the plane carrying the Pope was diverted to Naples due to a snow storm at Rome airport. The papal entourage arrived in Naples in the middle of the night. The elderly cardinal archbishop of the city was awoken and went to see the Pope who had been accompanied to the railway station in the hopes of arranging a train to Rome. Having flown from sweltering heat to frozen Italy, the Pope was wrapped in a blanket. "I know what the baby Jesus felt like," he quipped to the astonished cardinal.

The papal trips could be fraught with danger. In 1982, while visiting Africa, bad weather forced the papal plane to land in South Africa. The Pope had often expressed his disdain for apartheid, but during the two hour forced visit, he simply thanked the government for their hospitality. Travellers were surprised to see thePope crossing the Terminal with government officials

Pope John Paul greets the crowds at Knock, at the end of his visit to Ireland in 1979.

Africa held a particular fascination for Pope John Paul. He was enchanted by the vigour and vibrancy of its Catholicism and encouraged the rapid growth of Catholicism on the continent. In particular, he enjoyed the rhythmic music and stayed for hours at the colourful ceremonies.

The Pope learned a great deal during the visits. Many complained that they were ephemeral, and failed to engage in a meaningful way. Yet they brought the papacy into the global arena. Occasionally flashpoints arose. The Pope became more aware of priests involved in politics, and in some countries holding public office. During a visit to El Salvador in 1983, he berated Fr Ernesto Cardenal on the tarmac of the airport for not obeying a decree to leave the government of which he was a Minister. As the cleric knelt to kiss his ring, the Pope wagged his finger and told him to regularise his position within the Church.

The Pope was not consistent. He gace tacit support to Fr Jerzy Popieluszko, who opposed the Communist authorities. After the young nationalist priest was murdered, Pope John Paul presided over his beatification.

When challenged by the Holy See, the clergy involved in politics vainly protested that they did so as a means to improve the lot of the people, in the face of dictatorships or corrupt regimes. The Pope argued that the political area properly belonged to the lay faithful and was part of their distinct apostolate. Despite his political astuteness, Pope John Paul saw no paradox in the manner in which he forbade clerics to engage in politics while he waded headlong into complex diplomatic situations. Such actions were rejected by his critics as autocratic.

While the Pope generally received an enthusiastic welcome during the visits, many bishops believed that the trips undermined their local authority and further centralised the power of Rome. The Pope himself occasionally struck a severe tone when he addressed the local Bishops' Conference, criticising the direction of some projects while reprimanding the Bishops for not fitting into his vision of a perfect episcopate. These bishops rarely objected publicly, but they let their concerns be known, usually when the Pope had departed their shores.

Given the Vatican's geographical situation, there were also visits within Italy, some 144, not including those in Rome. The Italian visits were to the great cities, the shrines and remote areas. Again and again Pope John Paul addressed social and ethical issues, challenging Catholics and politicians alike regarding the manner in which they approached highly sensitive issues.

As bishop of Rome, the Pope undertook a systematic visitation of the capital's parishes. Shortly after his election, Pope John Paul met with Cardinal Poletti, the Vicar of Rome. The cardinal was charged with the day to day running of the diocese. The Pope explained that he would like to visit the parishes of Rome. The cardinal expressed his delight and promised he would choose one for him. The Pope explained that he intended to visit them all, not just one. The cardinal was taken aback, as no pontiff had ever carried out a systematic visitation of the parishes. When he explained that there were almost three hundred, the Pope replied that he hoped to be around for a long time.

Sunday after Sunday for quarter of a century, he toured the parishes, celebrating Mass and meeting the catechists, teachers, clergy, pastoral assistants and various groups. He visited on average about 15 each year. When he left the Vatican by car, he did not speak to his assistants until he arrived at his destination. It was part of his habit of silence prior to celebrating Mass.

Following his practice in Krakow, the Pope revived the Corpus Christi processions in Rome. Having celebrated Mass before the Cathedral of St John Lateran, the Pope brought the Blessed Sacrament in procession to St Mary Major Basilica, one mile away. Thousands took part in the colourful ceremony.

For all the artistic beauty of the historical centre of the city, many of the suburbs of Rome are hideous, and the quality of life is poor. His presence in a particular zone sometimes highlighted the problems of the area, and embarrassed local authorities to intervene with improvement schemes. In preparation for the Jubilee of 2000, the Pope visited a parish and visited some families in their homes, bringing them copy of the Gospels.

By the time of his death, Pope John Paul had visited 317 of Rome's 333 parishes. This did not account for the visits to convents and seminaries within the city.

On the Wednesdays before the Sunday visit, the Pope invited the clergy of the parish to lunch with him. He listened attentively as they described the reality of parish life, the obstacles, hopes and disappointments. In particular, he was interested in hearing about initiatives for young people. The visits served both encourage the parishioners and to give new heart to the priests and deacons who served them. From the start of his pontificate, the Polish pontiff had won over many Romans. Speaking from the balcony of St Peter's Square, the newly-elected pontiff had asked the people's indulgence: "If I make mistakes in your – no, our language. If I do, correct me." His mispronunciation of the word correct caused ripples of mirth and applause.

During his pontificate, John Paul II received more than 17 million people during some 1160 General Audiences. To this number can be added tens of millions who saw him at liturgies in Rome and throughout the world. His message was often challenging and uncompromising. His long speeches were not understood by all, nor did his listeners take his advice on many social and sexual issues. Yet for many, the Pope managed to reach out and touch each individual mind and heart. Even his most trenchant critics conceded that he had an extraordinary charisma rarely seen in the world.

John Paul and Ecumenism

Speaking in the Sistine Chapel on the morning following his election, Pope John Paul expressed his commitment to ecumenism, the search for Christian unity. Coming from a predominantly Catholic country, Karol Wojtyla had had relatively little exposure to the vast array of Christian denominations. The bishops meeting during the Second Vatican Council had given hope for the reunion between the Churches and various Christian communions. Pope John Paul committed himself to the dialogue, although many found his words contradicted his gestures.

In 1988, the Pope established the Pontifical Council for Christian Unity which fosters dialogue with all the non-Catholic Churches. During his apostolic journeys, he met with as many leaders of other Christian denominations as possible. These personal meetings, and the preparations, were designed to encourage understanding and trust. Writing in his Apostolic Letter, *Ut Unum Sint*, the Pope expressed his satisfaction with progress made to date. "At times it seems that we are closer to being able finally to seal this 'real although not yet full' communion. A century ago who could even have imagined such a thing?" He also expressed willingness for the Holy See to re-examine the way in which the Petrine ministry could be better expressed to rebuild unity.

Orthodoxy

Of all the branches of Christianity, Catholicism and Orthodoxy have most in common. Although separated for almost a thousand years, both Churches have made enormous strides in the past half century to achieve unity of practice and worship.

Pope John Paul made several gestures to improve relations between the Catholic Church and the Orthodox Churches

In 1964, Pope Paul VI and Athenagoras I, the Patriarch of Constantinople, met together in a historic encounter in Jerusalem. The symbolic embrace by the two men ended close on a millennium of mutual hostility. In 1054, relations between Rome and Constantinople deteriorated, as much due to political bickering as doctrinal disagreements. Both sides issued decrees of excommunication. The censure resulted in the rupture of communion which lasted until 1965.

JOHN PAUL AND ECUMENISM

Pope John Paul expressed his desire to unite the two churches across the map of Europe, so that the Church could "breathe once more with two lungs." As a Slav, he was in a unique position to contribute to this dream.

Culturally, he was close to Orthodox traditions and spirituality. His veneration of the saints, and above all of Mary, mother of Jesus, gave him an insight into the relationship of the Orthodox with Eternity. His personal experiences of the Second World War and subsequent Communist conquest of Eastern Europe forged a political link with Orthodox Christians in Russia who had shared a similar fate. However, the tortuous history of the Cold War era made Russians and Poles mutually suspicious of each other.

Significantly, Pope John Paul's overtures were resisted by Orthodox authorities, who were suspicious that the Polish Pope intended to absorb the very Churches which had struggled to survive under atheistic Communist regimes. Many saw the Catholic Church as part of the wealthy, consumerist West that wanted to liberate Eastern Europe.

Although Moscow remained for John Paul the ultimate, if unrealised, goal in his rapprochement with the Orthodox world, many initiatives successfully bore fruit. In May, 1999, the Pope visited Romania at the invitation of Theoctist, Patriarch of the Romanian Orthodox Church. It was the first time he had been invited to visit a predominantly Orthodox country. Welcoming his visitor, Theoctist noted that as the second millennium of Christianity began in schism, the beginning of the third promised healing and unity. In a gesture of friendship, the Patriarch of Constantinople, Bartholomew I, travelled to Romania to greet the Pope. The pontiff attended a Divine Liturgy celebrated by the Patriarch who also attended an open-air Mass which Pope John Paul celebrated. The Pope welcomed the visit as "a longed-for spring after a harsh and unrelenting winter."

In 2001, the Pope pushed further East, becoming the first

Pope in 1029 years to visit Greece. Several of the Popes of the first three centuries were Greek or Greek-speaking.

Welcomed by Archbishop Christodoulos of the Greek Orthodox Church, the Pope offered an apology for the Crusades which had ruptured links between the two Churches. In particular, the Pope acknowledged that the violent sacking of Constantinople in 1204 had led to centuries of distrust.

The closest Pope John Paul II came to visiting the heartland of the Russias was a trip to the Ukraine in June 2001. Two bishops of Rome had come from the Ukraine, St Clement I in the first century and St Martin I in the 7th century. Already in 1988, John Paul had celebrated Mass in St Peter's Basilica at the Vatican to mark the millennium of the Christianisation of Russia. The visit had been overshadowed by the Pope's desire to erect dioceses in Russia. The Orthodox opposed the project and threatened to boycott the visit.

Ukraine has a large number of Catholics who celebrate the Divine Liturgy according to the Byzantine Rite. Rather than acting as a bridge, the status of the Ukrainian Church threatened relations between the two Churches. Speaking in Kiev, the Pope expressed his delight at having overcome so many obstacles. Here he was able to celebrate the Divine Liturgy in the Byzantine Ukrainian rite. He noted that just a year after the millennium celebrations of 1988, the Berlin Wall was toppled, allowing the Christian faith once more flourish in the East. On that occasion, he also beatified Bishop Mykola Carneckhyj and twenty four companions, victims of totalitarian martyrdom and Nazism.

Cordial relations established over years with the Orthodox were almost undone in 2002 when the Pope erected several dioceses in Russia. Moscow was raised to the status of archdiocese and three other dioceses were created in Novosibirsk, Saratov, and Irkutsk. Orthodox authorities in Moscow dispatched envoys to the Vatican to protest at the action of the Holy See. In part, the Orthodox resented the reorganisation of

Catholics in territories which had for so long belonged to the Orthodox Church and which they had laboriously defended during the antagonistic Post-Revolution era. In part, the Orthodox regarded the 750,000 Catholics (0.5% of the population) as aliens.

The Pope's last gesture of reconciliation with Orthodox before he died was to return a copy of an icon of Our Lady of Kazan to Russia. According to legend, the icon had been discovered by a young girl, Matrona, on 8 July 1579. It was placed in a monastery in Kazan, a city built at the confluence of the Volga and Kazanka rivers. The icon had been venerated in the monastery church until its theft in 1904.

Following the Russian Revolution in 1917, there was speculation that the icon, along with many other religious artifacts, had been smuggled out of Russia to Fatima. In 1993, an 18th century copy of the icon was given as a gift to Pope John Paul, who kept it in his private chapel. The Pope often said that he would bring the sacred image to Russia, when he was permitted to make the long-wished for pastoral visit. "It was to accompany me for eleven years," he noted in August 2004, when he finally gave up the idea of travelling to Russia. "I prayed before the image which accompanied me daily in my service to the Universal Church." A year later, three months after the pontiff's death, the icon was enshrined in the Cathedral of the Annunciation in Kazan by the Patriarch of Moscow, Alexius II.

A visible sign of the improved relations came at Pope John Paul's funeral. At the end of the obsequies, before the Final Commendation, several Orthodox bishops joined other Christian leaders in praying around the funeral casket, offering liturgical chants and incensing the mortal remains.

The Reformed Churches

Following the Second Vatican Council, the Holy See engaged with a number of Reformed Churches in dialogue with the aim of eventual union. Between 1970-81, the Catholic Church and Anglican Communion engaged in a series of studies, called ARCIC I, which culminated in agreed statements on Ministry and the Eucharist. A second agreement, ARCIC II, was concluded at the end of the pontificate. On 31 October 1999, the Holy See and the World Lutheran Federation signed an agreed declaration on the issue of Justification by Faith.

The publication of the document *Dominus Iesus*, in September 2000 was seen by many as a severe setback to the ecumenical movement. The document, signed by Cardinal Joseph Ratzinger, underlined the differences between the Catholic and Reformed Churches as well as with world religions. It sparked furious reaction among many members of the Reformed Churches, who found both the language and content demeaning and condescending. The Pope had to try to mend fences. Speaking at the Angelus address a few days after the publication of the document, Pope John Paul said, "The document expresses once again the same ecumenical passion that is the basis of my encyclical *Ut Unum Sint*. I hope this declaration, which is close to my heart, can, after so many erroneous interpretations, finally fulfill its function both of clarification and openness."

Pope John Paul and Dr Ronald Runcie, the Archbishop of Canterbury met several times and fostered ecumenical dialogue

For John Paul, honesty in confronting differences was seen as more helpful than pretending differences did not exist. One particular issue was the decision of the Anglican and branches of the Reformed Churches to ordain women as deaconesses, priests and bishops. For John Paul, this proved to be a particular stumbling block. The Pope addressed the issue in his Apostolic Letter, *Ordinatio Sacerdotalis*, published at Pentecost 1994. Having surveyed the arguments for and against, he concluded "the Church has no authority whatsoever to confer priestly ordination on women and that this judgment is to be definitively held by all the Church's faithful." He moreover forbade any further discussion of the issue.

On a personal level, the Pope continued to build good relations with members of the Reformed Churches. He gave gifts of episcopal rings and pectoral crosses to Anglicans, despite the fact that the Holy See officially regarded Anglican Orders as "null and void."

The publication of the Catechism of the Catholic Church in 1995 was an attempt to provide an authoritative compendium of Catholic doctrine, and to replace a number of national catechisms, many of which were regarded by the Holy See as defective.

The period following the Second Vatican Council was marked by profound turbulence. The initial enthusiasm generated by the Council, its hopes and aspirations were left largely unfulfilled. A number of theologians, such as Hans Kung, Charles Curran, Paul Collins to record but a few, had their permission to teach in Catholic university faculties revoked. The writings of the popular Anthony de Mello were subject to criticism, eleven years after the author's death.

Even a Catholic archbishop was silenced. In 1983, Archbishop Raymond Hunthausen of Seattle was investigated for laxity in teaching the sexual ethics of the Church, especially regarding his pastoral care for homosexuals. While he was briefly replaced by Bishop Donald Wurl in 1985, he was restored two years later.

When Archbishop Emmanuel Milingo of Zambia contracted marriage in a ceremony performed by the Rev. Sun Moon of the Unification Church, the Pope urged him to return to ministry. Although the bishop obeyed, in 2006 he incurred automatic excommunication when he ordained four men without papal mandate. The Vatican treated Milingo with special attention as he had a large following in Africa, and the Holy See feared a schism.

Despite his traditional background, Pope John Paul was to preside over the only schism of the 20th century. Following the Second Vatican Council, a retired French missionary bishop, Marcel Lefebvre, opposed a number of the decrees. Despite the fact that he had participated in the Council, he rejected the final documents. In particular, the bishop disagreed with the Council's teaching on religious liberty and ecumenism. In 1970, Archbishop Lefebvre founded the Society of Pius X, opening a seminary in the Swiss town of Écône the following year. In 1976, he proceeded with the ordination of a number of deacons, leading to his suspension from celebrating the Sacraments. The prelate ignored protests from the Holy See and continued to train seminarians according to traditional theology. He also refused to embrace the liturgical reforms implemented by Pope Paul VI.

Intense dialogue followed with the Holy See, but the traditionalist bishop determined to consecrate four bishops to continue his ministry. Cardinal Joseph Ratzinger was designated by the Pope to lead efforts to reconcile the group. Proceeding to consecrate the bishops without papal mandate, the archbishop, his co-consecrators and the newly ordained bishops incurred the penalty of excommunication. But even following the rupture, the Pope continued to keep channels open, designating cardinals to maintain dialogue with the dissident clergy.

The Pope
and the Jews

Pope John Paul II was an eyewitness to the Holocaust in which some 9 million people died. Of this number, 6 million were Jews. Members of his own circle of friends were among the victims. In 1920, there were some 8,000 Catholics and 2,000 Jews in Wadowice. There was no segregation of Jews and both religions lived in close proximity to each other. The majority of the Jews were poor, even by the standards of early 20th century Poland. There was anti-semitism in his town, and as a child he heard jokes which debased his Jewish neighbours.

The official position of the Catholic Church in Poland was also anti-semitic. When Karol was 16, he heard a Pastoral Letter read in church. The Primate, Cardinal Hlond expressed his view as to why anti-semitism existed. "There will be a Jewish problem as long as the Jews remain...It is a fact that the Jews are fighting the Catholic Church, persisting in free thinking, and are the vanguard of godlessness, Bolshevism and subversion...It is a fact that the Jews deceive, levy interest and are pimps. It is a fact that the religious and ethical influence of the Jewish young people on Polish people is a negative one."

As a young boy, Karol had socialised with Jews, even though the Jews of the town largely preferred to keep to themselves. They had known generations of anti-semitism. Children can be unknowing and cruel conduits in perpetuating prejudices they little understand. Karol was fortunate that as a young boy he became acquainted with a family which inspired respect for the Jewish faith.

The Klugers were a wealthy family and owned substantial property in the town. Jerzy, who was the same age as Karol, also attended the same school and both boys shared a passion for football. The boys met when they were five and their friendship flourished. They were in class together and they visited each other's houses. The boys listened as Karol's father told them tales of the heroes of ancient Greece and Rome and Poland's warriors, and Karol often listened to music in the Klugers' home where two Jews and two Catholics met weekly to play string quartet music.

By the time Karol and his father moved to Warsaw in 1938, anti-semitism had deepened. Fanned by Nazi propaganda and prejudice, Poles began to accuse Jews of unpatriotic behaviour. In September 1939, the German army invaded Poland and the two countries were hurled into the Second World War. The Nazis destroyed the synagogue of Wadowice and forced the Jews to live in a ghetto. Jerzy Kluger and his father left the town to join the Allied forces. Jerzy was sent to Egypt and then on to fight the Nazis in Italy. Jews were deported to Auschwitz , amongst them Jerzy Kluger's mother and sister. After a lengthy incarceration, they died in the camp.

Karol and his father saw Jews herded into the ghetto, an area which was to be entirely destroyed by the Nazis in March 1943. When the Nazis invaded Warsaw, they closed the university and deported Jewish members of the faculty to the concentration camp of Sachsenhausen-Oranienburg

There are stories of Karol's attempts to help individuals. Edith Schiere was a girl who had been in a concentration camp.

After the war, she wanted to flee Krakow. As she was walking along the street, she fell to the ground from exhaustion. The newly ordained Fr Wojtyla happened to be passing at the moment. He stopped and bent down to help her. The emaciated girl explained that she simply wanted to leave the city, and the young man carried her to the train station.

Most Poles tried to ignore the Holocaust taking place around them. Karol was shocked and traumatised by the scale of the extermination of the Jews. He attempted in whatever way he could to help those in need.

In 1965, Jerzy Kluger read in a newspaper of an intervention of the Archbishop of Krakow at the Second Vatican Council. He had lost contact with most of his family and friends in Poland. He was surprised to know that his childhood friend was still alive. Kluger had settled in Rome and married an Irish Catholic wife. He managed to trace Karol who was staying at the Polish College in Rome. He phoned the College, wondering if Karol would recognise him after the passage of so many years. Although Wotyla was not in the College at the time he phoned, his call was returned that evening. Karol was surprised and delighted to hear from his friend and the two arranged to meet immediately.

Their newly kindled friendship, matured by time and experience, was to take on a deeper significance not only for them but for the relationship between Jews and Catholics worldwide.

At the time Archbishop Wotyla was taken up with the millennium celebrations of Poland's conversion to Christianity in 1966 and there was precious little time to see his friend in Rome. The two had to content themselves with telephone conversations and meetings during Wotyla's brief trips to Rome.

Over the next decade the two rebuilt their friendship, as Jerzy returned to Krakow to visit places he had not seen since his youth. Immediately after his election, the Polish Pope gave his first official audience to Jerzy and his family. Both tacitly realised the contribution they could make to eradicating anti-Semitism.

Those plans, which needed time to develop, were almost cut short by the assassination attempt on the Pope's life on 13 May 1981. Visiting his old friend in the Gemelli Polyclinic, Jerzy Kluger told the Pope that he brought greetings from scores of Jewish well-wishers. Some months later, during his convalescence, Kluger visited the Pope in Castelgandolfo. The Pope confided in him his plans to improve relations between Catholics and Jews. "You have to help me," the Pope said. "We need to proceed officially and unofficially. It will be a long road."

Kluger agreed to cooperate with his friend. Both men knew that an important step would be to establish full diplomatic relations with the State of Israel. The arduous task would require years of patience. The stumbling block was not just Israel, but also the Palestinian Authority. There was constant and violent friction between the two political bodies concerning borders. The Holy See supported the idea of a homeland for the Palestinians, many of whom had lived in makeshift accommodation for decades. It was necessary to convince both parties that the Holy See would act impartially to assist both.

While discussing a planned papal visit to America, the Pope asked Kluger if it would be appropriate to visit a synagogue. The Pope recalled that he had made his first visit to a synagogue in Krakow in February 1969 while visiting the parish of Corpus Domini in the Kazimerz district. It had been a spontaneous visit, but for several years, the Rabbi and Archbishop continued to exchange annual greetings.

Kluger thought for a while before replying. "It would make more sense if you, as Pope, visited the synagogue of Rome first." The Pope immediately agreed.

Between 1555 and 1870 the Jews of Rome had lived in cramped quarters in the shadow of the Theatre of Marcellus on the banks of the Tiber. Here they were forced to live behind high walls, leaving only during daytime to work in the city. On the sabbath, they were obliged to listen to sermons delivered by Catholic clergy, and at the election of a new Pope, the Jews had to lay the Torah on the ground before him. Only in the early 20th century were the Jews permitted to build their synagogue.

No Pope in two thousand years had made the short journey from St Peter's to the synagogue, just over a mile away. Yet the efforts to bridge the chasm required enormous patience. There was deep seated animosity and prejudice on both sides.

Rabbi Elio Toaff welcomes Pope John Paul following his first visit to Rome's synagogue in 1986

When Jerzy Kluger made contact with Elio Toaff, the elderly Chief Rabbi, he received a warm response. But Toaff warned him that the Synagogue Council might not be so positive. In the event, he was proved right, and only his sincere efforts and wise counselling prevailed on some members from boycotting the visit.

On 13 April, 1986, the Pope left the Vatican and seven minutes later, his car pulled into the courtyard in front of the Great Synagogue. Dressed in a white and blue prayer shawl, Rabbi Toaff embraced his guest warmly on the steps of the imposing edifice, which had been completed just over eighty years earlier. The pontiff greeted each person whom he met with the Hebrew word *shalom*, the greeting of peace. The Pope smiled broadly, although he was clearly nervous. Inside the congregation of 1,000 guests broke into spontaneous applause as the male voice choir sang from the 150th psalm, *Praise the Lord in his Holy place.*

The two men moved slowly down the aisle, before taking their place on two gilt chairs set on a blue carpeted dais in front of the shrine of the Torah.

In a brief address, the Pope replied to Rabbi Toaff's warm greetings. Reiterating the words of Pope John XXIII and the Vatican Council, he referred to the Jews as "our elder brothers," with whom God had established an irrevocable covenant. He deplored the centuries of persecution and venom which had marked the past two thousand years. Many were disappointed that he made no mention of the State of Israel. This visit, he explained, was first and foremost to the Jewish community living in Rome. But its repercussions were felt afar.

One of the fruits of the visit was the development of a personal friendship between Rabbi Toaff and the Pope. The rabbi would become a regular visitor to the Papal Apartments, and in his will the rabbi was the only person besides his Polish secretary whom John Paul II specifically mentioned.

The role of Jerzy Kluger continued to be vital as he worked in the background, often hosting informal lunches between Vatican and Israeli officials in his tennis club. These convivial meetings did not entirely overcome differences. There were tensions over the Holy See's good relations with the Palestinian Authority and over tax issues of properties belonging to the Church in the Holy Land.

On 7 April, 1994, Pope John Paul hosted a concert in the Paul VI Audience Hall, commemorating the Holocaust. Seated beside him was Rabbi Toaff. The conductor was Jewish, Gilbert Levine, who for some years had directed the Krakow Philharmonic Orchestra. The Pope understood that music is an art which transcends all borders and had asked Levine to assist in his project to improve Catholic and Jewish relations.

In 1998, the Pontifical Council for Inter Religious Dialogue issued a document under the Pope's direction commemorating the Shoah and deploring the "crime which is a stain on the history of the century."

The Pope committed himself and the Church to the eradication of anti-Semitism. "We have seen with our eyes, we were and are witnesses of violence and hatred, which are kindled in the world all too often and consume it. We have seen and we see peace derided, brotherhood mocked, harmony ignored, mercy scorned."

On the occasion of his pilgrimage to the Holy Land in 2000, the Pope made two iconic visits. The first was to the memorial in honour of the victims of the Shoah at Yad Vashem. When he met with some survivors of the Shoah, he was astonished to meet the woman whom he had carried to the station over fifty-four years earlier. At the end of the visit, the Pope thanked Jerzy Kluger. "Your name will be remembered in history, and honoured for what you have done."

While praying before the Wailing Wall at the Temple in Jerusalem, the Pope took a sheet of paper from his pocket. Using a cane, he shuffled painfully to the wall. Following the practice of many Jews, he placed the paper in a crevice between the bricks. With his head bowed, he prayed in silence. After he had left, some curious viewers took the paper to read. The pontiff had composed a brief prayer:.

"God of our fathers, you chose Abraham and his descendants to bring your name to the Nations: we are deeply saddened by the behaviour of those who in the course of history have caused these children of yours to suffer, and asking your forgiveness we wish to commit ourselves to genuine brotherhood with the people of the Covenant. Through Jesus, the Christ, our Lord. Amen".

The words and sentiments rang all the truer from the hand of a Pole who had lived through the horrors of the war and seen the devastation caused by human hatred.

The Pope continued to foster the improving relations between Catholics and Jews, although he also strenuously defended the rights of the Palestinians to their political security. Fittingly, the last Private Audience the Pope gave before he died was to a delegation of 138 Jewish leaders. They had come to the Vatican on the tenth anniversary of the establishment of diplomatic ties with the State of Israel.

On 1 April, 2005, the day before the Sabbath and as Pope John Paul was dying, Rome's chief rabbi, Riccardo Di Segni, went to St Peter's Square. "I have come" he said, "to pray here in the piazza as a sign of sharing in the grief of our brothers, for their concerns and as a sign of warmth for this Pope and for all that he has done.'

John Paul and Religions of the World

During the Second Vatican Council, the Catholic Church examined its relationship with world religions. Where the emphasis had always been to convert people to Christianity, the bishops acknowledged the presence of God in all humanity. This positive approach allowed new links to be forged in the post- conciliar years. Pope Paul VI, more than any modern Pope was particularly sensitive to the beauty and depth of non-Christian religions.

The 20th century saw a rapid expansion in the number of Christians in the world. At the beginning of the century, there were some 558 million Christians globally. By the end of the century, that number had risen to 2 billion. This resulted from a combination of missionary activity by all the main churches as well as a dramatic population explosion.

While Christians made up 34.5 % of the world's population in 1900, by 2004 it was just 33.1%. Christianity arrived in Latin American and parts of West Africa with the Spanish and Portuguese conquests of the 15th and 16th century. Today, much of the hegemony of the Catholic Church has been undermined by the growth of Pentecostal and independent churches.

Pope John Paul understood that social communications were becoming ever more sophisticated. While some 28 % of Christians lived in cities at the turn of the 20th century, by the end of his pontificate that number had risen to 58%. The Pastoral Visits, often criticised as little more than a brief flash of papal power, were also efforts by the Pope to engage in dialogue with other cultures. It was the responsibility of the local bishops, he claimed, to build on any achievements gained by the papal visits.

John Paul was the pontiff *par excellence* of grand gestures. On 27 October, 1986, he invited Christian leaders and representatives of the world's major religions to a forum held in the Umbrian town of Assisi. During his travels around the globe, the Pope had become increasingly aware of both the positive and negative role religions can play in society. Inaugurating a World Day of Prayer for Peace, he encouraged world leaders to join together to promote harmony:

"With the world religions we share a common respect for and obedience to conscience, which teaches all of us to seek the truth, to love and serve all individuals and people, and therefore to make peace among nations."

As they gathered in the Square of the Lower Basilica of St Francis, each religious leader or representative was presented with a miniature olive tree, a biblical symbol of peace. In his efforts to establish common ground between Catholics and members of other world faiths, the Pope was assisted by members of the Sant' Egidio Community, which since its foundation in 1968 had fostered dialogue between world religions.

In the years following the Assisi gathering the Community organised international meetings. In 1989, the Community sponsored a gathering in Warsaw, observing the 50th anniversary of the beginning of World War II. The meeting of 1995 took place in Jerusalem, with the title, "Jerusalem, City of Peace for Jews, Christians and Muslims."

Karol Wojtyla grew in his knowledge and appreciation of various religions during his trips. Given his Polish background, he had little contact with members of other religions. That was to change when he became Pope.

Speaking at Mass in New Delhi on 7 November 1999, the Pope explained his reason for coming to India, where the majority of the population was Hindu and Muslim "I come to you as a pilgrim of peace. My presence among you is a sign that the Catholic Church wants to enter a dialogue with the religions of the world."

The largest non-Christian religion in the world is Islam. At the beginning of the 21st century, Muslims – numbering 1.2 billion followers – had outstripped Catholics, numbering 1.1 billion. In the Declaration, *Nostra Aetate*, the bishops attending the Second Vatican Council expressed their respect for Islam. "The Church has a high regard for Muslims. They worship God, who is one, living and subsistent, merciful and almighty, the Creator of heaven and earth, who has also spoken to men. They strive to submit themselves without reserve to the hidden decrees of God, just as Abraham submitted himself to God's plan, to whose faith Muslims eagerly link their own. Although not acknowledging him as God, they venerate Jesus as a prophet; his virgin Mother they also honour, and even at times devoutly invoke. Further, they await the Day of Judgment and the reward of God following the resurrection of the dead. For this reason they highly esteem an upright life and worship God, especially by way of prayer, alms-deeds and fasting".

Where possible during pastoral visits, the Pope paid a courtesy call on Muslim authorities, and each year a message was sent to the Islamic world to mark the holy month of Ramadan.

The relationship of the Catholic Church with Islam took a dramatic turn following the tragic attacks on the World Trade

Representatives of world religions gather in the Church of St Mary of the Angels at Assisi in 1986

Centre on 11 September 2001. The Pope was in Castelgandolfo the morning the news broke. He watched incredulously the live television reports and spent much of the day in the chapel. Despite centuries of mutual suspicion between the Church and Islam, Pope John Paul repeated continuously his desire that peace triumph over religious division. Speaking to religious leaders some weeks after the offensive on 18 November 2001 the Pope said, "We wish to have Christians and Muslims come together to proclaim before the world that religion must never be a reason for conflict, hatred and violence...in this historic moment, humanity needs to see gestures of peace and to hear words of hope" As ever a man of gesture, Pope John Paul decided to convene a second World Day of Prayer for Peace. Inviting leaders of all world religions to Assisi, the Pope hoped such a move would grasp the attention of the world's media.

On 24 January, 2002, the Pope set out by train from the Vatican for Assisi. Accompanying the pontiff were various faith leaders and as the train passed on its journey people waved their encouragement. The gesture captured the mood of the people for whom the world had radically changed following the terrorist attacks in America.

Once again the town of St Francis was to host leaders of all faiths. Some 200 leaders accepted the Pope's invitation. Each would pray in their own tradition, invoking God to change the hearts of violent and evil people. Prominent among the leaders were 29 senior clerics from Saudi Arabia, Libya, Egypt, Iran, Iraq, Morocco and Tunisia. Cardinal Joseph Ratzinger had publicly expressed his disapproval of the 1986 meeting, where religious leaders prayed together. However, he gave tacit consent to the second pilgrimage when he was assured that each religious leader was to be accorded his or her own space in which to pray. Syncretism, in Joseph Ratzinger's view, was both dishonest to all religions and harmful to Catholics. Freedom to choose various parts from religions and mix them with Catholicism was ultimately a betrayal of Jesus. Nothing could justify a false reconciliation.

Although John Paul respected the various religions in the world, he was also acutely aware of the tensions between them. In many countries Christians suffered at the hands of religious fanatics. During weekly meetings with bishops from all over the world, the Pope regularly heard about persecution of Christians by Hindus and Muslims among others. According to the Bishop of Rumbek in Sudan, Monsignor Caesare Mazzolari, three million Catholics took refuge in the north of the country to find employment and political asylum. In order to obtain these, they were obliged to become Muslims, making the *shahada*, or public profession of faith.

The Pope had the delicate task of defending his flock and deflecting violence against them. During his pastoral visits, he made impassioned pleas for the rights of Catholics in lands governed by *sharia* law and asserted the rights of Christians to worship in freedom. Islam required careful attention. The year following his election, Pope John Paul travelled to Turkey, a lay State where Islam is the majority religion. In 1985, he became the first Pope to visit a Muslim country, the Kingdom of Morocco, at the invitation of a Muslim leader. In 2001, he received his first invitation to visit a mosque, the Umayyad Mosque in Damascus.

John Paul expressed a controversial view of Buddhism in his book *Crossing the Threshold of Hope*, published in 1994. He saw Buddhism more as a philosophy than a religion. While Christianity sees the destiny of humanity as eternal life, Buddhism teaches that the ultimate aim of the human being is *nirvana*, or a state of annihilation. These views caused controversy although the Pope maintained good relations with Buddhist leaders such as the Dalai Lama.

The document *Dominus Iesus,* published in 2001, reaffirmed the Church's missionary role which some felt had been played down in the second half of the 20th century.

Regarding the relation of Christians with other faiths, the document cautioned against seeing one religion as good as another. The document reasserted the special position of the Church in the world "If it is true that the followers of other religions can receive divine grace, it is also certain that objectively speaking they are in a gravely deficient situation in comparison with those who, in the Church, have the fullness of the means of salvation."

Despite this reservation, the quarter century of John Paul's pontificate led to a greater understanding between the Church and other world faiths.

John Paul and Young People

The day after his election, Pope John Paul II went to visit his life-long friend Bishop Andrej Deskur at the Gemelli Hospital. The two Poles had come to know each other in the 1940s when both were studying for the priesthood in Krakow. Deskur, now a bishop in the Roman Curia, had suffered a crippling stroke. The incapacitated bishop lay paralysed in the bed. The Pope took his hand and encouraged him. "You got me here, now you have to get better."

When he took his leave, he saluted the medical staff which had gathered along the corridors, mesmerised that the newly elected Pope was in their midst. Realising that he was beside a ward with sick children, he asked if he could visit them.

The Pope was ushered into the ward. Although most were too sick or young to recognise their illustrious visitor, they responded to the man in white who went around each bed, blessing and kissing each child. Although the visit lasted only a few minutes, it deeply impressed all. None had seen such an interaction before. For John Paul it was natural.

John Paul was always relaxed in the company of children. A little girl is embraced during a visit to Africa.

As he made his way to the exit, a crowd had gathered. The Vatican security force was insufficient for the people who excitedly jostled him and pushed The Pope to the floor. As one of the guards apologised, the Pope smiled and said, "We must get used to it."

This first contact with children and young people was to last throughout the pontiff's lifetime.

Five days later, as the Mass of Inauguration drew to a close, the concelebrants filed towards the entrance of St Peter's Basilica. It had been a long ceremony, filled with emotion for all who had witnessed it.

The new pontiff was not ready to leave the out-door sanctuary. Grasping his pastoral cross, he strode down the steps towards the vast crowd which thronged the piazza. Flags waved and enthusiastic voices were raised. "Viva il Papa!"

As hands stretched out to touch him, he bent over and blessed some people in wheelchairs. As he turned to join the procession, a young boy broke from his guardians. Suddenly realising that he was alone, he stopped. The Pope saw him, and walked over to the child. Taking his hand, he accompanied him back towards the crowd, searching for the child's parents or guardians.

During the summer holidays, the Pope began a practice of inviting young people to visit with him in the gardens of

The Pope greets children following the Mass of Pentecost in St Peter's Square

Castelgandolfo. Twice a week at 9.00 pm, the Pope left the villa and entered the gardens. The meetings were informal. Seated on a wicker chair with young people around him, the Pope was entirely relaxed. He often would lead them in singing songs, and the more extrovert young people would engage him in discussion or even perform tricks. The meetings generally lasted one or two hours but they were gatherings which the papal villas had never seen before.

During every Pastoral Visit, the Pope requested the host country to organise an encounter with youth. During a visit to Paris, the Pope met young people at the *Parc des Invalides*. As the young people responded to his words, they sprang to their feet in an alternating Mexican Wave. A young man tried to ask him a question. In the vast crowd, it was impossible to hear what the youth was saying. When he returned to Paris, the Pope wrote to Cardinal Marty, the Archbishop of Paris. He promised to write to the young man and answer his question privately. It was to give the Pope an idea which found its fruition some years later in World Youth Day

At Galway in Ireland, he celebrated Mass with thousands of young people from all over Ireland and beyond. As he delivered his homily, he paused and said "Young people of Ireland. I love you!" The words had a dramatic effect. The Pope had expressed his closeness and they responded with spontaneous applause, singing and chanting, which lasted seventeen minutes. Despite his efforts to continue, the pontiff finally put his speech to one side and joined in the singing.

As a young priest, Karol Wojtyla gathered his young students into a *Srodowisko*, a encounter group where members could explore the meaning of their lives and reflect on their value - system. Under Communist rule in Poland, Church sponsored youth- gatherings were frowned upon. Working as a university chaplain and later as a professor, the young priest organised expeditions to the mountains where they could spend time together in dialogue. In order not to draw the attention of state

The Pope receives a warm welcome from children as he visits one of the parishes in Rome.

police, he wore lay clothes and requested his students to call him Uncle. Even as Cardinal, many of his friends continued to call him by the affectionate term.

Reflecting upon the success of the youth meetings in each country which he visited, Pope John Paul began to plan an international congress. He had seen groups such as *Pueri Cantores*, members of children's choirs gather together for international conventions. With a small group of collaborators drawn from the Curia, he laid plans for an international meeting to be hosted in Rome.

The first two meetings took place in the Vatican at Easter 1984 and 1985. Over quarter of a million attended each festival. At Christmas 1985, the Pope decided that the World Youth Day would become an annual event, with alternative years celebrated in the local diocese. In 1987, the third World Youth Day was held in Argentina, and the Pope travelled for the event. Over a million young people attended. By 1995, the festival had been spread over a week and in Manilla, where more than 4 million people attended the papal Mass, the largest religious gathering in human history took place.

As the years passed by, Pope John Paul was unable to participate as before. No longer could he command the crowd with a word, a silent pause, a single gesture. Seated on his chair, he lifted his hands and began to sway them from side to side. Almost crippled with arthritis, he was determined to join his young friends as best he could. His face was suffused with delight, drawing energy as always from the enthusiastic response. Speaking to Spanish youths in Madrid in May, 2003, he quipped "I am a young person aged 83."

Although the Pope had undeniable gifts of communicating with youth, his knowledge of their needs and aspirations was largely academic. He had no nieces or nephews, and only very distant cousins. The majority of the young people whom he met on a social basis were children of long-time friends, mostly Polish. Often he was their host and they were deferential to him.

Occasionally, during youth rallies, questions and views would be laid before him. These, however, were usually filtered through layers of Curial vetting and the result was innocuous. Cardinal Ratzinger revealed his embarrassment when a welcome from a young person during a papal visit to Munich went against what had been prepared. A young person charged to give a welcome address made critical remarks on the state of the Church. Pope John Paul considered dissension debilitating and discussion of many issues taboo.

Despite the hardships of his own youth, he viewed the years of his childhood and adolescence with nostalgia. But there was an enormous generational gap. The pleasures of mountaineering and canoeing contrasted dramatically with the modern world of discos and unfettered freedom. John Paul found it difficult to understand a culture where abortion had become a means of regulating the family and where contraception was available on an industrial scale. While some young people had access to great riches, the majority lived in poverty. Mass communication displayed unequivocally to all the needs of humanity as the globe shrank to the size of a village.

Sometimes he cajoled his young listeners, other times he railed against such hedonism. But his world view was moulded in the grey, jagged years of the Second World War and its ensuing distress and privation. An implacable opponent of atheistic Communism, he was equally dismayed by the Capitalism of the West which so carelessly squandered the communal resources of the planet.

But the message was normally delivered with good humoured banter. He did not seek to flatter his young audience, nor prey on their insecurities. John Paul II was convinced that the Gospel message was a cornucopia, filled with rich things to guide young people as they made their way into mature adulthood.

In New York, he listened to young people chant "John Paul Two – We love you!" He hummed along for a few minutes before responding to them. "I also have a song. It is this: John Paul Two – He loves you!"

Starting in Poland, young people began the habit of serenading the Pope under his bedroom window at the end of each day. The Pope normally appeared for a few minutes to bless them. These sometimes turned into prolonged impromptu meetings, as Pope and youths sang together. "Now go to bed," he pretended to scold them. "You may have nothing to do tomorrow, but I have to work!"

From his days as chaplain to young people in the parish of St Florian to his tenure as lecturer in philosophy at Lublin University, Karol Wojtlya had a particular appreciation for university students. He challenged their views and offered paternal advice as no other Pope had done. He inaugurated an annual Mass to open the academic year at the Roman universities. He enlisted the young people to use their intellectual prowess to assist their peers and evangelise them.

One of his last great youth rallies was at Tor Vergata in August, 2000. It was the Jubilee Year and the Pope had invited the youth of the world to make a pilgrimage to the tombs of St Peter and St Paul. There was no space large enough in the city centre, so an area near Rome's newest university in the suburbs was designated to receive the hundreds of thousands who poured into the Eternal City.

At a Prayer Vigil on the evening before World Youth Day , the Pope met with the enthusiastic crowd. It was a sweltering Roman evening. Although he was physically frail, he still commanded their attention. As the crowd burst into the theme song, *Jesus Christ, You Are My Life*, the Pope pretended to conduct them. He burst out laughing on several occasions, as he beamed out over the faces of two million young people.

A teenage boy broke from group behind the pontiff and ran to his chair. Members of the Vatican security personnel were not

As he criss-crossed the globe, Pope John Paul took every opportunity to meet and encourage the youth of the world.

JOHN PAUL AND YOUNG PEOPLE

quick enough to stop him. Archbishop Piero Marini, the Master of Liturgical Ceremonies, was standing behind the Pope's chair and indicated to them that the boy meant no harm. The young boy knelt in front of the pontiff and whispered into his ear. For several minutes the youth poured out his heart to the Pope who nodded and embraced him.

After a while, the pulled the microphone to himself. "I knew you were here," he quipped, "even before I saw you. I heard you making this chaotic noise even in the helicopter." The crowd roared its approval. "And all Rome knows you are here! They can hear you all the way into the city centre. They will never forget you were here. The poor people! They are trying to sleep!"

During the last years of his pontificate the Pope continued to attend events with young people, and he always spoke to them in the context of the family. The World Day of the Family, an initiative he designed to strengthen the unity of the family in society, was an effort to encourage Catholics to live their Christian vocation together.

As he lay dying on Friday, April 1, 2005 the Pope listened to the voices of young people who prayed and sang hymns of comfort. When his secretary told him about the thousands filling the Square beneath his window, the old man asked for a piece of paper. Mouthing words without a voice, he wrote his last words.

"I sought you out and now you come to me. Thank you."

John Paul
and Mary

Choosing his episcopal motto, Karol Wojtyla quoted from the 17th-century French Saint Louis Marie Grignion de Montfort. The saint had written a book *True Devotion to the Blessed Virgin Mary*, expressing his love for Mary and his desire to dedicate himself entirely to her. The phrase *totus tuus*, entirely yours, expresses De Montforte and Wojtlya's filial and tender love of Mary.

When he was elected to the papacy, John Paul insisted on inserting the letter M for Mary on his shield. The papal armourist, Archbishop Bruno Heim, politely objected that this broke with heraldic tradition, but the newly elected Pope insisted.

Since his youth, Karol Wojtyla regularly wrote an invocation to Mary at the top of each sheet. As Pope, he concluded every speech and homily with an invocation and prayer to the Blessed Virgin. During his pastoral visits, the Pope went to shrines of Mary. On 13 May, 1982, the Pope visited the shrine of Fatima in Portugal, where many believed that the Blessed Virgin had appeared to three children in 1917. The Pope had

The Pope kneels in prayer before a shrine of Mary the mother of God. In every country he visited, he always made a pilgrimage to a Marian shrine

made the visit on the first anniversary of the dramatic assassination attempt in St Peter's Square. As he mused on the manner in which he had escaped death, he said "while one hand fired the bullet, another hand guided it." For him, there was no doubt. Since he had lost his mother in childhood, Mary had become a spiritual surrogate mother.

Inspired by Mary's care for the Church, the Pope publicly consecrated the Church and the world to Mary's maternal care during a ceremony on 8 December 1990.

As a young man, Karol had met a mystic called Jan Tyranowski, who led an apostolate called the "Living Rosary." Regarded by many as an eccentric, Karol was enthralled by his devotion to Mary. Tyranowiski gathered a couple of dozen young people around him and imbued them with a deep devotion to Mary. He also introduced them to the writings of St John of the Cross. Around this time he began to wear a brown woolen scapular, squares of cloths held by strings on the back and chest. This scapular he wore until the day of his death.

Karol Wojtyla recited the Rosary several times each day of his life. To mark the 25th year of his pontificate, John Paul II introduced a new set of prayers in the Rosary, called the "Mysteries of Light." These biblical meditations expanded the traditional devotions in honour of Jesus and Mary.

In the years following the Second Vatican Council, popular piety and devotion to Mary had diminished. On 25 March 1987, Pope John Paul II published an encyclical, *Redemptoris Mater*. In it the Pope explored the close relationship of Mary to her son and her relationship with the Church. The year corresponded with the 12th centenary of the Second Council of Nicea and inaugurated a "Marian Year," designed by the pontiff to deepen understanding of Mary's role as the help of Christians. The fact that it concluded in the 14th centenary of the baptism of the Russias was seen by the Slavic pontiff as a providential opportunity to draw closer to the Orthodox Churches of the East. It was a magisterial document but it was aimed also at rebalancing Catholic's attitude to Mary. The letter was deeply embedded in Sacred Scripture, but it also pointed the way in which Mary could assist Christians attain unity of prayer and worship.

The Marian Year was also designed to celebrate the 2000 anniversary of the birth of the Blessed Virgin Mary. During his years in Krakow, he had accompanied the ikon of the Black Madonna to each of his parishes. The Marian year was an effort to reach out to Christians and help them deepen their understanding of Mary's role in the history of spiritual redemption.

The Pope was deeply impressed by apparitions of Mary and took a particular interest in reported visions at Medjugorje in Bosnia Herzcevogina, where visionaries claimed that Mary had begun to visit in the summer of 1981. Although the Pope never visited the shrine, he followed reports of the alleged visitation of the Blessed Virgin with great interest.

Karol Wojtyla had a particular devotion to Our Lady of Fatima, and during visits to the shrine at Portugal, he met with the Carmelite Sister Lucia, one of three children who claimed to have seen Mary in 1917. He also beatified the two other seers, Jacinta and Francisco Marto on 13 May 2000.

That same year, shortly before his 80th birthday, Pope John Paul authorised that a letter, written by Sr. Lucia in 1944, be published. The letter, sometimes referred to as the Third Secret of Fatima, pointed to the assassination of a bishop. Although Sr. Lucia did not indicate it was Pope John Paul, the pontiff himself believed it was a reference to the assassination attempts made on him.

Twice Pope John Paul visited Lourdes, in 1986 and 2005. On the latter visit, he sat for a long time alone before the Grotto when St Bernadette Soubrious claimed she had seen Mary in 1854. "Pray for me," he asked his fellow pilgrims. "I am old and sick."

John Paul's Social Teaching

In 1891 the aristocratic Leo XIII published a survey of the engagement of the Church and politics. During the 19th century, much of Europe had moved rapidly from a rural agricultural economy to an industrial urban society. People who had once made their living from the fruits of the land now found themselves herded into industrial slums where dreams of a better society lay shattered.

Leo's analysis of what went wrong with the promise of a better future laid the blame at the door of political structures. Condemning governments which treated citizens as items of the economy rather than individuals, Leo's ideas were refined in 1961 by Pope John XXIII in his encyclical *Mater et Magister* and two years later, in the encyclical *Pacem in Terris*. Pope John spoke from first hand experience of the grind of life. His own father was a farmer. "There are three ways a man can be ruined," he once remarked. "Gambling, women and farming. My father chose the most boring!"

Karol Wojtyla was the first pontiff in centuries who had struggled to earn a wage and had lived through the dramatic

upheaval of a world war. He had dealt at first hand with an oppressive Communist regime which was determined to marginalise the Church in Polish society. The Poland of his formative years was poor and in childhood he was used to living frugally. Conditions deteriorated dramatically in the Second World War and its aftermath. Karol lived simply with little interest in possessions. His contemporaries recall how he wore clothes until they were threadbare.

When Pope John Paul wrote about social justice, his words struck an authentic chord with many. During a visit to a slum in Brazil, he took off the gold ring on his finger and gave it to the bishop to sell on behalf of the poor. In the early part of his pontificate, he came into conflict with a socio-theological movement, Liberation Theology, which stressed a "preferential option for the poor."

Pope John Paul was dismayed to learn how many clergy were leading revolutionary groups. He opposed strands in Liberation Theology which professed to do away with clerical hierarchy. He argued that the proponents confused the sacramental role of the priest with that of a social reformer.

The theologian Leonardo Boff was critical of John Paul's approach to the Latin American Church, asserting that "the Vatican wants a stronger Church, not a better world." Yet, despite his firm disapproval of some developments in Latin America, nobody could mistake his genuine concern for the needs of the poor and their rights. Again and again, he challenged dictatorships which undermined the needs of poor people. His vision demanded that all people enjoy fundamental rights, including freedom and work. For John Paul, work was not something to be endured. Rather it was to be celebrated in itself, cooperating with the Creator.

Pope John Paul had an enormous respect for Mother Teresa of Calcutta

Pope John Paul stoutly defended the traditional Christian view of the world, especially in the area of sexual ethics. Increasingly, he found himself a lone voice in his opposition to what he perceived as mistaken forms of sexual liberation.

JOHN PAUL'S SOCIAL TEACHING

In 1985, Pope John Paul was due to make a visit to the Cameroon. Meeting with advisors, he asked them for ideas about his speeches. One advisor told him that his view was too idealistic. Slavery began in the country, he argued, and the Pope needed to address that fact. The Pope admitted that he did not know much about slavery. He was given a biography of Bartolomé de las Casas, the 15th-century defender of Indian and African slaves. The Pope had never heard of the Dominican friar, and deeply appreciated the insights of the reformer. His lengthy speech to the President, Government and Diplomatic Corps in Yaoundé, showed a deep understanding of the challenges of sub-Saharan Africa as it struggles to emerge from centuries of exploitation.

In order to help the Africans of the Sahel, Pope John Paul set up a foundation, which finances the efforts of Africans to help themselves out of poverty. He donated whatever monies he received from his writings and pensions.

One of the most influential people on Pope John Paul was Mother Teresa of Calcutta. The diminutive nun, founder of the Missionaries of Charity, had spent years working with the poor and destitute in the slums of Calcutta. Pope John Paul visited her in India in 1986 and every time she came to Rome she called to see the Pope. In 1988, Pope John Paul and Mother Teresa opened a hostel, *Dono di Maria*. The hostel, set into the walls of the Vatican, today offers 74 beds for women, and daily meals and clothing services for those in need.

The Pope was highly appreciative of the effort of religious Sisters and Brothers and the vast array of lay volunteers in the works of charity. Some quarter of the people living with HIV AIDS are cared for by Catholic institutions. The Catholic Church has had a long involvement in health and education. These are tools for eradicating poverty and ensuring that people can live with dignity. Pope John Paul summed up his life's thinking on the need for justice human rights in his encyclical *Laborem Exercens*, published in 1981. Just months earlier,

Polish shipyard workers had called a general strike as they established the first Trade Union within the Soviet bloc. Led by an electrician, Lech Walensa, the group called itself Solidarity.

In Rome the Pope watched anxiously as the government imposed martial law in order to quell the counterrevolutionary ideals. In his speeches, he assured his fellow-Poles of his support in their efforts to establish trade unions. The Solidarity group became a vital force in Polish politics and Walensa eventually was elected President of Poland. This moral backing was instrumental in the break-up of Soviet bloc countries and the eventual unification between east and west. The American President Ronald Reagan tacitly assisted the Polish pontiff's efforts, and later claimed that the Polish pontiff was responsible for the collapse of Communism in Eastern Europe.

John Paul and Suffering

The latter years of John Paul's life were marked by evident physical and psychological suffering. His intense patriotism made him feel the dramatic events unfolding in his homeland all the more. Following the Second World War, Germany and Poland were partitioned in a manner which deeply affected the national psyche. Polish Catholics often felt that theirs was a Church of Silence where the West failed to understand the enormous sacrifices demanded of Catholics as they strove to remain faithful to the Church.

This sense of isolation often led to a personal sense of loss. Karol Wojtyla's youth was marked by the Second World War. Yet despite these difficulties and, deprivations the young man's health was robust. Despite all his work-related commitments, he never neglected physical exercise, canoeing, skiing, hiking and swimming.

The most dramatic event of Karol Wojtyla's life took place on 13 May 1981. Shortly before the General Audience was due to begin at 5.30 p.m, the Pope entered St Peter's Square in a

Pope John Paul enters the Nervi Hall for a General Audience. No longer able to walk unaided, the Pope nevertheless insisted on keeping his regular appointments

white open- top jeep. As the vehicle approached the podium in front of the Basilica, several shots rang out. The Pope felt a sharp pain in his hand and abdomen. Looking down at his white soutane, he fell backwards as blood began to seep through the cloth. The jeep reversed, racing back behind the Basilica. The Pope was now slumped against his secretary Father Stanislaw Dziwisz.

The Pope had been hit four times, twice in the abdomen, once in his left hand and in his right arm. As he fainted, he was lifted into an ambulance. Despite the traffic, the ambulance raced to the Gemelli Polyclinic, arriving less than ten minutes later.

The Pope had lost nearly three quarters of his blood and needed emergency transfusions. That night he underwent a six-hour operation on his intestines and peripheral wounds.

Meanwhile the gunman, Mehmet Ali Aga, had been wrestled to the ground by Camillo Cibin, the head of security and some pilgrims. Two women, from New York and Jamaica, had also been injured and were attended to immediately in the hospital. Aga was apprehended and consigned to the care of Italian police. Two months later, he was sentenced to life imprisonment.

Writing of the dramatic events in his book *Memory and Identity*, Pope John Paul said that Aga was a professional assassin and therefore he followed the orders given by others. He explained that he trusted he would not die. "I had a feeling that I would survive. I was in pain. I had reason to be afraid, but I had this strange feeling of confidence. Oh my Lord! This was a difficult experience!"

Some weeks later, the Pope entered hospital once more to reverse a temporary colostomy which had been inserted during the 13 May surgery.

The following year, on the anniversary of the attempt on his life, the Pope made a pilgrimage of thanksgiving to the shrine of Our Lady at Fatima. The Pope was attacked by a deranged priest, Fr Juan Maria Ferdinez, who stabbed him with a dagger. The wound was superficial, and the Pope did not need surgical attention.

In 1983, Pope John Paul travelled to the Rebibbia Prison where Aga was detained. When asked why he made the visit, the Pope replied that Jesus urged his followers to visit those who are in prison.

A year later, Pope John Paul wrote an Apostolic Letter, *Salvifici Doloris*. Dated 11 February, the Feast of Our Lady of Lourdes, it was a meditation on the spiritual effects of mental and physical suffering. In the 17,000 word document, the Pope analysed suffering as a common experience of all life, but one which binds humans closer together. Ultimately, the Pope saw suffering as supernatural, but also as a means of refining and purifying genuine love. For those who read it, the pontiff's words were underscored by his own physical and psychological pain. But the path of suffering was to become ever steeper.

On Sunday 12 July 1992, Pope John Paul announced at the noon day Angelus that he would enter the Gemelli Polyclinic that afternoon. Three days later, following tests, the 72-year old pontiff was operated on for a benign tumour in the stomach. He was hospitalised for three weeks.

The previous year, he had noticed a slight tremor in his hands. It was most visible when he held them up in prayer at Mass. The middle finger in his right hand had been injured in the 1981 assassination attempt, but the tremor was in both hands. During a routine check-up, Dr Renato Buzzonetti suggested that it might be little more than an age-related palsy.

The tremors progressed and by the following year, the Pope had developed difficulty in walking. He was now 73. Further tests indicated that the Pope may have developed Parkinson's disease, an illness caused by the loss of dopamine in the brain and which controls limb movements. Although this was a visibly progressive disease, the Pope and his advisors saw no need to publicise his illness. The Pope began to take medication, but he soon realised that there was little hope of a cure.

For some years the Pope had been suffering from ankylosing spondylitis, a painful form of arthritis which affected his spine and gave him a hunched aspect. His height shrunk from 5.10 to 5.8 inches. In November, as he was leaving an audience in the Hall of Benedictions in St Peter's façade, the Pope slipped on a newly installed carpet. He fell down three steps and fractured his right shoulder. But his trials were not over.

On Christmas Day, as he read his greetings in several languages from his study window, he was forced to break off mid-sentence. He had been suffering with influenza and had been confined to bed. A vomiting bug had taken its toll and left him debilitated. The greetings were broadcast live throughout the world, and for the first time people saw the Pope extremely ill.

Five months later, on 30 April, Pope John Paul slipped in the bathroom one evening. He had taken a shower and as he emerged, he slipped and fractured his femur.

Admitted to the Gemelli Polyclinic once more, he was operated on and a metal prosthesis was inserted. "You have to admire my loyalty," the Pope wryly quipped as he was admitted to hospital for the sixth time. By now he had spent 105 days of his 15 year pontificate in the hospital. Despite the technical success, the Pope was left with a painful limp, which added to the increasing discomfort caused by Parkinson's disease.

The last major operation was for appendicitis. For most of the year he had suffered episodes of pain associated with an inflamed appendix. Having beatified a number of blessed on Sunday 4 October, the Pope was admitted that afternoon to the Gemelli Polyclinic. Two days later his appendix was removed.

The Pope's condition continued to worsen. Rumours that he was suffering from Parkinson 's disease continued to abound although the Vatican officially denied it until 2003. By now, the Pope had great difficulty walking. In 1998, John Paul began to

The elderly pontiff greets children during
Mass in the Sistine Chapel on the Feast of
the Baptism of the Lord.

JOHN PAUL AND SUFFERING

use a motorised buggy along the corridors of the Vatican. When his assistant told him that such buggies were used at airports, the Pope sat into the rubber- wheeled car. "Next stop," he said, "is Miami."

With the progression of his illness, his speech became slurred as his facial muscles were affected by the syndrome. John Paul was determined to preside over the events of the Great Jubilee of the year 2000, reminiscent of the success of the Millennium of Polish Christianity in 1966.

But by now the Pope was a semi-invalid. While reading homilies, he struggled to form the words, and often his listeners were unable to understand what he was saying. The remaining years of his pontificate were marked by a slow physical decline.

On 10 January 2004, the Pope released two doves from the window of his studying during the noon-day Angelus. Although he spoke a few words, the paralysis of his facial and throat muscles meant his words were unintelligible. He had contracted the flu, and for the next few days he remained in bed.

On 1 February 2005, the Pope was admitted to the Gemelli late one evening. He had begun to have difficulty swallowing during his meal; he began to choke and the doctor was summoned immediately. The Pope was rushed to hospital where he recovered from the incident. In an unusual public display, he left hospital in the evening of 10 February and was driven to the Vatican in an illuminated Popemobile.

While at dinner on the evening of 23 February with his lifelong friend Cardinal Marian Jaworski, the Pope had another attack. The cardinal was so startled that he wanted to administer the Sacrament of the Sick immediately to his old friend. The Pope was put to bed but as his condition worsened during the night, it was decided to admit him once more to the Gemelli hospital the next morning.

The decision was taken to perform a tracheotomy to ease his breathing. The Pope was asked for his permission. He inquired if it would be possible to have the operation during the summer holidays. The doctors explained the urgency. Dr Buzzonetti leaned over and assured him that it would be a simple operation. To which the Pope replied with a wry smile, "Easy for whom?"

After the operation, he discovered that his voice was gone. He had not fully realised the danger that he might lose the power of speech and was bitterly disappointed. Asking for a piece of paper, he wrote: "what have you done to me?" He then wrote the words Totus Tuus.

On 13 March, he returned to the Vatican to recuperate. It was close to Easter and for the first time in his 26-year pontificate cardinals were delegated to celebrate the Easter ceremonies. On Good Friday, a TV link showed the Pope seated in his private Chapel, watching the Stations of the Cross relayed from the Colliseum. He clutched a cross to his chest. Those who saw and heard the Pope in those days knew that the end was drawing near.

The death of Pope John Paul

On Easter Sunday, the Pope insisted on appearing at the window of his Private Apartments to greet the thousands who had gathered in prayerful support. At the end of the Mass celebrated in the piazza by Cardinal Sodano the Pope was due to address the crowds. As a microphone was placed before him, he struggled to speak, but only guttural gasps reverberated around the public address system. People in the crowd began to cry openly as they witnessed the great communicator reduced to silence. In frustration, he hit his forehead with the palm of his hand, tracing the sign of the cross three times over the crowds. As he was wheeled back into his room, he began to weep.

On Wednesday 30 March, the Pope came to the window once more to greet five thousand children who had come from the

Archdiocese of Milan. Again he was unable to speak and simply blessed the youths in silence. The next morning at 11 am, while preparing for Mass in his chapel, the Pope suffered a septic shock. He began to shake uncontrollably and he was wheeled from the chapel to his bedroom.

By now the pontiff's temperature was 40 degrees. There was no question of returning to hospital. "If it is time for me to die," he said, "let me die here." It was clear to Dr Buzzonetti that this was the patient's most serious episode, the result of a urinary tract infection. According to a Polish custom, a single candle was lit by the bedside. The death vigil had begun. The cardinals and close friends were summoned to the Papal Apartments to make their personal farewells. Cardinal Ratzinger recalled how the Pope was no longer able to speak, but shook hands and gave him his blessing.

Throughout the following day, people quietly entered the bedroom where the Pope was drifting in and out of consciousness. In the late afternoon, the Pope tried to speak. Sr Tobiana bent to hear his words. "Let me go to the Lord," he whispered. Among those in the room was Wanda Poltawska. The two had been friends for 55 years. When Wanda was diagnosed with cancer in 1962, Cardinal Wojtyla wrote to the mystic Capuchin Padre Pio requesting prayers. Some weeks later, the Cardinal wrote to Padre Pio again, informing him of her miraculous cure.

Overcome with emotion, Sr Tobiana ran from the room. Shortly afterwards, around 7.00 pm, the Pope fell into a coma. Bishop Stanislaw began to celebrate the Vigil Mass of Divine Mercy, in the bedroom. The Pope had canonised the Polish nun Sr Faustina and had established the Feast of Divine Mercy. Down in the piazza, the sound of singing and the Rosary drifted up on the night air. Thousands held candles in the vigil for the Bishop of Rome's last journey.

The life of this extraordinary man was coming to its end. An actor, a stone cutter, a philosopher, a poet, a teacher, a priest.

No Pope had ever had such a varied life as John Paul II.

Shortly after Mass, at 9.37, the Pope stopped breathing. There was a silence in the room as those gathered around the bedside realised that the Pope had died. Led by bishop Stanislaw, spontaneously , the small group of Sisters and friends began to sing the *Te Deum* of Thanksgiving.

In the piazza below Archbishop Leonardo Sandri, Substitute at the Secretariat of State, interrupted the recitation of the Rosary to announce to the crowds. "The Holy Father has gone to the House of the Eternal Father."

The Funeral of Pope John Paul

Although prepared for an outpouring of grief, the Vatican could not have foreseen the public reaction to the death of Pope John Paul II. For over twenty-six years he had dominated the Church and was one of the most familiar faces on the planet.

Cardinal Eduardo Somalo Martinez, Camerlengo of the Church, now took charge as the *sede vacante* began. He defaced the Ring of the Fisherman, the papal seal, to prevent any documents been forged during the interregum. The Dean of the College of Cardinals, Joseph Ratzinger, convened the cardinals to Rome for the conclave to elect a new Pope.

The body of the Pope, vested in a red chasuble and his pastoral staff in the crook of his arm, was laid out in his private chapel, the heart of his home. A simple white mitre was placed on his head, and his white woolen pallium embroidered with black crosses, was laid over his shoulders.

Throughout the night, the Pope's secretaries and his immediate household kept vigil around the body.

The following day the Pope's remains were placed on a bier and brought to the Sala Clementina in the Apostolic Palace for

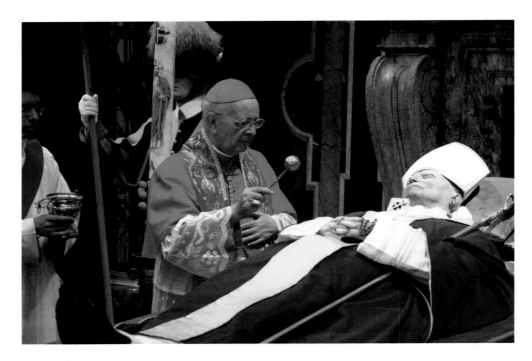

Cardinal Eduardo Somalo Martinez blesses the corpse of the deceased pontiff at the beginning of the lying-in-state in the Clementine Hall

all his close collaborators to make their farewell. Swiss Guards stood in attendance as prayers were recited by the Cardinal Camerlengo.

The next day, the body was brought in procession down the Scala Regia, the royal staircase designed by Bernini in 1666. Friars and clergy preceded the bier, chanting the litany of the Saints in Latin. As the cortege entered St Peter's Square, the thousands took up the plea, *Ora pro nobis* – saints of God, pray for us, pray for him. On the steps of St Peter's Basilica, the prayers for the dead were recited before the pontiff's body was accompanied into the church, where it was placed before the High Altar.

For four days, millions of Romans and pilgrims filed past the body of the Pope. Queues stretched along the Tiber, up the Via Della Conciliazione and into the side streets, before entering the Square. Many waited up to six or eight hours to pay their final respects.

The Pope's funeral Mass was celebrated on 8 April. It was a

blustery day, and as the coffin of the pontiff was brought from the Basilica onto the sagrato in front of the facade, the crowd burst into applause. The ushers carried the coffin to the centre of the platform, where it was laid on the ground before the Altar. A red-bound copy of the Gospels was placed on the coffin. As the concelebrating cardinals took their places, the cover of the book blew open. For the entire Mass, the wind ruffled the pages of the Gospel book.

During his homily, the chief celebrant Cardinal Ratzinger recalled the last days of the pontiff's life.

"None of us can ever forget how in that last Easter Sunday of his life, the Holy Father, marked by suffering, came once more to the window of the Apostolic Palace and one last time gave his blessing *Urbi et Orbi* – to the city and the world. We can be sure that our beloved Pope is standing today at the window of the Father's house, that he sees us and blesses us. Yes, bless us, Holy Father. We entrust your dear soul to the Mother of God, your Mother, who guided you each day and who will guide you now to the eternal glory of her Son, our Lord Jesus Christ."

As the Mass ended, some people in the crowd unfurled flags with the words Santo Subito – Make him a saint immediately. Shouts began to resound around the Piazza. A saint immediately.

As the coffin was carried up the steps to enter the Basilica for internment, the ushers turned the coffin once more to face the crowds. On the balcony overhead he had begun his public ministry twenty-six and a half years earlier. "Be not afraid," he had said on this spot on the day of his inauguration, "throw open the doors to Christ, for he knows what is within us!"

As the coffin was borne into the darkness of the Basilica, the people in the crowd waved their final farewell. The Pope had gone home to the house of the Father.

The Beatification of Pope John Paul II

In his letter to the early Christian community at Corinth, St Paul urges the followers of Christ to be saints (1 Cor.1-2) The call to sanctity is central to the Christian vocation. Paul meant holy in the terms of pious, devoted to God and living a life worthy of the gift of baptism.

In subsequent centuries, Christians came to regarded the saints as exemplars of the Faith. For the most part, the term saint means one who has lived a heroically Christian life and is now believed to be in heaven. For Paul, everyone without exception was called to live an unblemished life.

In past centuries, Christians honoured in a particular way members of the community who had died and were venerated as radiant reflections of perfect fidelity to Jesus.

From the beginning of the Christian faith, many faced persecution and even violent death. Following the example of Jesus, they chose to imitate the manner in which he died. They were in turn honoured by the Christian community as martyrs, from the Greek word to witness. Their unwavering faith in Jesus earned them the gratitude and admiration of generations of Christians.

By the 4th century, as the era of imperial persecutions passed, Christians continued to hold up the example of those whose lives were memorable by their charity, forbearance and piety.

Although often a person was acclaimed a saint *vox populi* – through the spontaneous voice of the people – soon a process arose whereby the life of the deceased was examined in the local diocese. If they passed scrutiny, they were held up as exemplars in the faith. Such investigations and their results were local. A feast day was instituted and a public cult began. Only with the permission of the bishop could the veneration be expanded into neighbouring dioceses. In theological terms, the word veneration is important. Saints are not worshipped, simply honoured.

In the Middle Ages, devotion to local *beati* spread. Tombs of the deceased often became pilgrimage sites, with attendant complications. It was not uncommon for unscrupulous people to exploit the innocent faith of pilgrims. The Church developed forms to examine the lives and in some cases the teachings of the deceased and around whose memory a cult had developed. From the 11th century, the Popes recommended that veneration of the saints be confided to General Councils. In 1234, Pope Gregory IX laid down regulations and established procedures to examine cults. In particular, claims to miraculous healings were scrutinised.

In 1588, Pope Sixtus V (1585-90) set up a special commission, the Congregation of Rites (later the Congregation for the Causes of the Saints) to oversee the entire process whereby the local cult of a "blessed" could be extended to the whole Church. In such a case, the "blessed" was declared a saint. In 1634, Pope Urban VIII (1623-44) confirmed that only the Holy See could authorise local and universal veneration, through the approved rites of beatification and canonisation.

The purpose of the investigation was to sift through the

evidence of holiness, separating exaggerated piety from sound doctrine. Witnesses were to be interviewed and writings and teachings carefully examined.

Today, the process remains much the same as laid down by Pope Urban but it was most recently reviewed by Pope John Paul II in 1983. The Polish pontiff had an extraordinary interest and personal devotion to the saints. During his long pontificate, he canonized 482 saints and beatified 1,342 people, more than all his predecessors combined. This was in part due to his lengthy pontificate and also due to the fact that Pope Paul VI had introduced a method of accelerating the beatification process. Pope Paul realised that it was more desirable to beatify people within living memory.

Following the death of a person "in the odour of sanctity," the bishop of the diocese where the person died may be petitioned by the faithful to open a canonical process. A period of five years must pass, simply to see if the euphoria dies away. The Pope has the authority to waive the five-year period as happened with the beatification of Mother Teresa of Calcutta and Pope John Paul II. Pope Benedict followed the exemption by opening the cause his predecessor's beatification a month after his death.

If a sufficient number of credible witnesses request the local bishop, the investigation commences. A postulator is appointed to oversee the beatification process. All written data is collected and witnesses, both for and against a beatification, are examined under oath. In particular, reports of miracles are examined. One hundred and fourteen people gave extensive interviews about the Karol Wojtyla whom they knew. Not all were positive. Although the witnesses gave testimony under oath, some had already expressed concern over his handling of the sexual abuse of children by clergy, and of his naivety concerning the founder of the Legionaries of Christ, Rev. Marcial Maciel Degollado, accused of sexual abuse and later condemned by Pope Benedict XVI in 2005.

Beatification is not about a person's judgement or defects. It is a decree that the venerated person, within their limits, lived a heroic life in the Catholic faith.

If the results are largely positive, the bishop commissions the officials to prepare a report, with all attendant documentation, which is sealed and sent to the Congregation for the Causes of the Saints. The candidate now is given the title "Servant of God." If the Prefect of the Congregation accepts the judgement of the bishop, he assigns a new commission. The task is to verify if the person may be honoured with the formal title "blessed."

A miracle is required before the official rite of beatification can take place. Many claims of cures due to the intercession of Pope John Paul II were examined by the commission before one was chosen. It concerned reports that a French nun, Sister Marie Simon-Pierre, who had been diagnosed with Parkinson's disease in 2001, was cured through Pope John Paul's intercession. She testified to the commission how the debilitating disease, from which the pontiff himself had suffered for thirteen years, had completely disappeared. In May 2005, the Sisters of her Order began to pray to the late Pope. When she awoke on the morning on 3 June, three months after the Pope's death, she was completely mobile. The previous evening her superior had tried to comfort her, saying, "Pope John Paul has not said the last word yet." The uncontrollable shaking had abated and she was able to walk unaided. Within weeks she resumed her full-time work as maternity nurse. A medical and religious commission reported that the cure appeared instantaneous and permanent.

The commission concluded its work in late 2010 and submitted its findings to Pope Benedict XVI. On 14 January, the Pope gave permission for the beatification to take place. In a break with his normal habit, the Bavarian-born pontiff and friend of Karol Wojtyla announced that he would preside at the beatification in St Peter's Square. It would be another important step for Blessed John Paul on the path to sainthood.

As hundreds of thousands of pilgrims from all over the world poured into Rome, the doors of welcome were thrown open.

The celebrations began with a Night Vigil at the Circus Maximus, ruins of a chariot track dating back to the 5th century BC. It lies between the Aventine and Palatine Hills, and here over half a million pilgrims took part in a candlelit prayer vigil organised by the Diocese of Rome.

The late Pope's secretary of 39 years, Cardinal Stanislaw Dswisz spoke movingly of his years of service at Karol Wojtyla's side. "People ask me about my memories, and in these days I am full of nostalgia. I am certainly not sad, but joyful. I know he is in heaven, but I feel his presence every moment of every day on earth."

Thousands of pilgrims joined in the Mass of Beatification on 1 May 2011.

The secretary, who had caught Pope John Paul as he fell victim to a would- be assassin's bullets on 13 May 1981, admitted that

most of his life had been spent with the Pope. "In all those years, I only left him for my annual vacation, and was at his side always. To serve Karol Wojtyla was to love his silence. He was totally immersed in God. He felt that he collaborated with God to achieve His work."

The thousands gathered listened intently to the French nun healed through the Pope's intercession as she explained: "I did not know the Pope personally, but I am in his debt for this miracle of healing."

The crowds watched as images of the late Pope's life were beamed on a large screen above the speaker's heads. In the second half, the swelling crowd prayed the Mysteries of Light, a decade of the Rosary which the late pontiff had added shortly before he died. There were satellite links to Marian shrines at Fatima, Guadalupe, Tanzania, Krakow and Lebanon. Pope Benedict also participated by visual link, imparting his blessing.

When the vigil ended, the crowds returned to their lodgings, singing hymns to Our Lady. Many made their way across the Tiber, where they camped in the streets outside the Vatican ready for the Mass. Churches remained open throughout the night, and offered hospitality to the hundreds who had arrived in Rome unable to find accommodation.

The weather had been unsettled in the days leading up to the ceremony and the day dawned with grey skies.

In the early hours of the morning, the barriers leading into the Square were opened to allow pilgrims take up their place for the ceremony.

By dawn it appeared that the rain clouds were blowing away. The entire square was now filled and the terraces of the Apostolic Palace overlooking the piazza were dotted with Vatican employees and some friends who crowded onto the space for a bird's eye view of the ceremony. Hundreds of thousands could not get near the Vatican and watched as the ceremony unfolded on enormous screens erected in the area.

Following the Mass of Beatification, Pope Benedict XVI prays before the coffin containing the remains of Blessed John Paul.

Two and a half thousand media personnel were present in Rome to follow the historic ceremony, the most rapid beatification in recent memory.

The procession began at 10. am. Eighty-seven delegations from various countries, among which were 5 royal houses, 16 heads of state – including the presidents of Poland and Italy – and 7 prime ministers, were seated on the platform in front of the Basilica.

Shortly after the great bell of the tower tolled, the choir began the Gregorian Chant *introit* and from the Bronze Door of the Apostolic Palace the papal procession began. Preceded by the cardinals and other concelebrants, Pope Benedict was brought by Popemobile through the crowds to the sanctuary set out on the top of the steps in front of the St. Peter's façade.

At the beginning of the Mass, Cardinal Vallini, the Vicar of Rome, made the formal petition to Pope Benedict to proclaim Pope John Paul blessed. After a short biography had been read, the Pope gave his consent. A roar rose from the thousands in the piazza and surrounding streets. As the choir broke into song, an image of Blessed John Paul was slowly unveiled above the balcony where he had first addressed the city and the world on the night of his election on 16 October 1978.

Two nuns went to present a relic of the late pontiff to Pope Benedict. A phial of blood, which had been extracted from the late Pope in hospital before his death, was placed in a silver reliquary beside the altar. One of the Sisters who carried the relic was Sr Tobiana, who had looked after Pope John Paul in the papal apartments for two decades. She had held his hand as he died and was the last person to whom the Pope spoke. The other nun was Sr Marie Pierre Simon Normand.

In his homily, Pope Benedict expressed his pleasure that the day of Pope John Paul's beatification had come so soon. He assuaged those who considered the process too hasty. Many were concerned the Pope John Paul had dealt with the abuse of children by clerics inadequately. In particular, the pontiff was criticised for not evaluating correctly the founder of the Legionaries of Christ, Fr Marcial Maciel Degollado, who had been punished by Pope Benedict for his duplicity and the abuse of minors. The Bavarian pontiff concluded with a personal reflection of the friend with whom he had worked since the Second Vatican Council.

"I would like to thank God for the gift of having worked for many years with Blessed Pope John Paul II. I had known him earlier and had esteemed him. I was at his side and came to revere him all the more. My own service was sustained by his spiritual depth and by the richness of his insights. His example of prayer continually impressed and edified me: he remained deeply united to God even amid the many demands of his ministry. Then too, there was his witness in suffering: the Lord gradually stripped him of everything, yet he remained ever a 'rock', as Christ desired. His profound humility, grounded in close union with Christ, enabled him to continue to lead the Church and to give to the world a message which became all the more eloquent as his physical strength declined. In this way he lived out in an extraordinary way the vocation of every priest and bishop to become completely one with Jesus, whom he daily receives and offers in the Eucharist."

At the end of the homily, the crowds were requested to furl their banners and not to applaud. The rest of the Mass continued in prayerful recollection.

Immediately after the Mass, the Basilica was opened. The previous day, the body of the pontiff had been exhumed and his coffin was now placed in front of the Altar of the Confession, above the tomb of Peter. Pope Benedict and the cardinals led the procession to venerate the remains of Blessed John Paul. Four Swiss Guard stood at each quarter of the coffin, which lay on a cloth of gold, surrounded by white and yellow roses. A copy of the Gospels lay open on the coffin.

For the rest of the day, throughout the night and into the following day, thousands of pilgrims filed past the coffin, which was surrounded by yellow and white flowers. On Monday 2 May the Cardinal Secretary of State, Cardinal Tarcisio Bertone, celebrated the Mass of Thanksgiving in the Square for quarter of a million people.

That evening, the coffin of the newly-blessed Pope John Paul was moved in procession to the Chapel of St Sebastian. The archpriest of the Basilica, Cardinal Comastri, led the small group which included the late Pope's secretaries and the nuns who cared for his household, as well as his medical staff. As they sang the Litany of the Saints, the small cortege arrived at the chapel.

His remains were entombed under the altar, which had until the previous month housed the relics of Blessed Pope Innocent XI. A white marble plaque sealed the opening, with the word inscribed Beatus Ioannes Paulus PP. II.

The first step on the road to sainthood had been completed. Now a new process began. People began to pray for a second miracle to take place after the beatification. When a new miracle would be verified, the last step would be ready. John Paul would be declared as saint and he would be venerated throughout the world.

Homily given by Pope Benedict XVI during the Mass of Beatification in St Peter's Square, 1 May 2011

Dear Brothers and Sisters,

Six years ago we gathered in this Square to celebrate the funeral of Pope John Paul II. Our grief at his loss was deep, but even greater was our sense of an immense grace which embraced Rome and the whole world: a grace which was in some way the fruit of my beloved predecessor's entire life, and especially of his witness in suffering. Even then we perceived the fragrance of his sanctity, and in any number of ways God's People showed their veneration for him. For this reason, with all due respect for the Church's canonical norms, I wanted his cause of beatification to move forward with reasonable haste. And now the longed-for day has come; it came quickly because this is what was pleasing to the Lord: John Paul II is blessed!

I would like to offer a cordial greeting to all of you who on this happy occasion have come in such great numbers to Rome from all over the world – cardinals, patriarchs of the Eastern Catholic Churches, brother bishops and priests, official delegations, ambassadors and civil authorities, consecrated men and women and lay faithful, and I extend that greeting to all those who join us by radio and television.

Today is the Second Sunday of Easter, which Blessed John Paul II entitled Divine Mercy Sunday. The date was chosen for today's celebration because, in God's providence, my predecessor died on the vigil of this feast. Today is also the first day of May, Mary's month, and the liturgical memorial of Saint Joseph the Worker. All these elements serve to enrich our prayer, they help us in our pilgrimage through time and space; but in heaven a very different celebration is taking place among the angels and saints! Even so, God is but one, and one too is Christ the Lord, who like a bridge joins earth to heaven. At this moment we feel closer than ever, sharing as it were in the liturgy of heaven.

"Blessed are those who have not seen and yet have come to believe" (Jn 20:29). In today's Gospel Jesus proclaims this beatitude: the beatitude of faith. For us, it is particularly striking because we are gathered to celebrate a beatification, but even more so because today the one proclaimed blessed is a Pope, a Successor of Peter, one who was called to

confirm his brethren in the faith. John Paul II is blessed because of his faith, a strong, generous and apostolic faith. We think at once of another beatitude: "Blessed are you, Simon, son of Jonah! For flesh and blood has not revealed this to you, but my Father in heaven" (Mt 16:17). What did our heavenly Father reveal to Simon? That Jesus is the Christ, the Son of the living God. Because of this faith, Simon becomes Peter, the rock on which Jesus can build his Church. The eternal beatitude of John Paul II, which today the Church rejoices to proclaim, is wholly contained in these sayings of Jesus: "Blessed are you, Simon" and "Blessed are those who have not seen and yet have come to believe!" It is the beatitude of faith, which John Paul II also received as a gift from God the Father for the building up of Christ's Church.

Our thoughts turn to yet another beatitude, one which appears in the Gospel before all others. It is the beatitude of the Virgin Mary, the Mother of the Redeemer. Mary, who had just conceived Jesus, was told by Saint Elizabeth: "Blessed is she who believed that there would be a fulfilment of what was spoken to her by the Lord" (Lk 1:45). The beatitude of faith has its model in Mary, and all of us rejoice that the beatification of John Paul II takes place on this first day of the month of Mary, beneath the maternal gaze of the one who by her faith sustained the faith of the Apostles and constantly sustains the faith of their successors, especially those called to occupy the Chair of Peter. Mary does not appear in the accounts of Christ's resurrection, yet hers is, as it were, a continual, hidden presence: she is the Mother to whom Jesus entrusted each of his disciples and the entire community. In particular we can see how Saint John and Saint Luke record the powerful, maternal presence of Mary in the passages preceding those read in today's Gospel and first reading. In the account of Jesus' death, Mary appears at the foot of the cross (Jn 19:25), and at the beginning of the Acts of the Apostles she is seen in the midst of the disciples gathered in prayer in the Upper Room (Acts 1:14).

Today's second reading also speaks to us of faith. Saint Peter himself, filled with spiritual enthusiasm, points out to the newly-baptized the reason for their hope and their joy. I like to think how in this passage, at the beginning of his First Letter, Peter does not use language of exhortation; instead, he states a fact. He writes: "you rejoice", and he adds: "you love him; and even though you do not see him now, you believe in him and rejoice with an indescribable and glorious joy, for you are receiving the outcome of your faith, the salvation of your souls" (1 Pet 1:6, 8-9). All these verbs are in the indicative, because a new reality has come about

HOMILY GIVEN BY POPE BENEDICT XVI

in Christ's resurrection, a reality to which faith opens the door. "This is the Lord's doing", says the Psalm (118:23), and "it is marvelous in our eyes", the eyes of faith.

Dear brothers and sisters, today our eyes behold, in the full spiritual light of the risen Christ, the beloved and revered figure of John Paul II. Today his name is added to the host of those whom he proclaimed saints and blesseds during the almost twenty-seven years of his pontificate, thereby forcefully emphasizing the universal vocation to the heights of the Christian life, to holiness, taught by the conciliar Constitution on the Church Lumen Gentium. All of us, as members of the people of God – bishops, priests, deacons, laity, men and women religious – are making our pilgrim way to the heavenly homeland where the Virgin Mary has preceded us, associated as she was in a unique and perfect way to the mystery of Christ and the Church. Karol Wojtyla took part in the Second Vatican Council, first as an auxiliary Bishop and then as Archbishop of Kraków. He was fully aware that the Council's decision to devote the last chapter of its Constitution on the Church to Mary meant that the Mother of the Redeemer is held up as an image and model of holiness for every Christian and for the entire Church. This was the theological vision which Blessed John Paul II discovered as a young man and subsequently maintained and deepened throughout his life. A vision which is expressed in the scriptural image of the crucified Christ with Mary, his Mother, at his side. This icon from the Gospel of John (19:25-27) was taken up in the episcopal and later the papal coat-of-arms of Karol Wojtyla: a golden cross with the letter "M" on the lower right and the motto "Totus tuus", drawn from the well-known words of Saint Louis Marie Grignion de Montfort in which Karol Wojtyłała found a guiding light for his life: "Totus tuus ego sum et omnia mea tua sunt. Accipio te in mea omnia. Praebe mihi cor tuum, Maria – I belong entirely to you, and all that I have is yours. I take you for my all. O Mary, give me your heart" (Treatise on True Devotion to the Blessed Virgin, 266).

In his Testament, the new Blessed wrote: "When, on 16 October 1978, the Conclave of Cardinals chose John Paul II, the Primate of Poland, Cardinal Stefan Wyszyński, said to me: 'The task of the new Pope will be to lead the Church into the Third Millennium'". And the Pope added: "I would like once again to express my gratitude to the Holy Spirit for the great gift of the Second Vatican Council, to which, together with the whole Church - and especially with the whole episcopate - I feel indebted. I am convinced that it will long be granted to the new generations to draw from the treasures that this Council of the twentieth century has lavished upon us. As a Bishop who took part in the Council from the first to the last day, I desire to entrust this great patrimony to all who are and will be called in the future to put it into practice. For my part, I thank the Eternal Shepherd, who has enabled me to serve this very great cause in the course of all the years of my Pontificate". And what is this "cause"? It is the same one that John Paul II presented during his first solemn Mass in Saint Peter's Square in the unforgettable words: "Do not be afraid! Open, open wide the doors to Christ!" What the newly-elected Pope asked of everyone, he was himself the first to do: society, culture, political and economic systems he opened up to Christ, turning back with the strength of a titan – a strength which came to him from God – a tide which appeared irreversible. By his witness of faith, love and apostolic courage, accompanied by great human charisma, this exemplary son of Poland helped believers throughout the world not to be afraid to be called Christian, to belong to the Church, to speak of the Gospel. In a word: he helped us not to fear the truth, because truth is the guarantee of liberty. To put it even more succinctly: he gave us the strength to believe in Christ, because Christ is Redemptor hominis, the Redeemer of man. This was the theme of his first encyclical, and the thread which runs though all the others.

When Karol Wojtyła ascended to the throne of Peter, he brought with him a deep understanding of the difference between Marxism and Christianity, based on their respective visions of man. This was his message: man is the way of the Church, and Christ is the way of man. With this message, which is the great legacy of the Second Vatican Council and of its "helmsman", the Servant of God Pope Paul VI, John Paul II led the People of God across the threshold of the Third Millennium, which thanks to Christ he was able to call "the threshold of hope". Throughout the long journey of preparation for the great Jubilee he directed Christianity once again to the future, the future of God, which transcends history while nonetheless directly affecting it. He rightly reclaimed for Christianity that impulse of hope which had in some sense faltered before Marxism and the ideology of progress. He restored to Christianity its true face as a religion of hope, to be lived in history in an "Advent" spirit, in a personal and communitarian existence directed to Christ, the fullness of humanity and the fulfillment of all our longings for justice and peace.

Finally, on a more personal note, I would like to thank God for the gift of having worked for many years with Blessed Pope John Paul II. I had known him earlier and had esteemed him, but for twenty-three years, beginning in 1982 after he called me to Rome to be Prefect of the

Congregation for the Doctrine of the Faith, I was at his side and came to revere him all the more. My own service was sustained by his spiritual depth and by the richness of his insights. His example of prayer continually impressed and edified me: he remained deeply united to God even amid the many demands of his ministry. Then too, there was his witness in suffering: the Lord gradually stripped him of everything, yet he remained ever a "rock", as Christ desired. His profound humility, grounded in close union with Christ, enabled him to continue to lead the Church and to give to the world a message which became all the more eloquent as his physical strength declined. In this way he lived out in an extraordinary way the vocation of every priest and bishop to become completely one with Jesus, whom he daily receives and offers in the Eucharist.

Blessed are you, beloved Pope John Paul II, because you believed! Continue, we implore you, to sustain from heaven the faith of God's people. Amen.

Prayer to implore favours through the intercession of Blessed John Paul II, Pope

O Blessed Trinity, we thank You for having graced the Church with Blessed John Paul II and for allowing the tenderness of Your Fatherly care, the glory of the Cross of Christ, and the splendour of the Spirit of love, to shine through him. Trusting fully in Your infinite mercy and in the maternal intercession of Mary, he has given us a living image of Jesus the Good Shepherd, and has shown us that holiness is the necessary measure of ordinary Christian life and is the way of achieving eternal communion with You. Grant us, by his intercession, and according to Your will, the graces we implore, hoping that he will soon be numbered among Your saints. Amen.

With ecclesiastical approval AGOSTINO CARD. VALLINI
Vicar General of His Holiness for the Diocese of Rome

Appendix 1

The Pope's Letter of Resignation

Following the example of Pope Paul VI, I declare,

In the case of illness, which will be presumed to be incurable, of long duration, and which would prevent me from adequately fulfilling the functions of my Apostolic ministry,

Or in the case of another serious and prolonged impairment,

I renounce my sacred and canonical office, both as Bishop of Rome and head of the Holy Catholic Church, confiding it to the Lord Cardinal Dean of the Sacred College of Cardinals, leaving to him, along with at least the Cardinals in charge of the Dicasteries of the Roman Curia, and with the Cardinal Vicar of Rome (providing they can come together to meet), or else to the Cardinal heads of the Sacred College, the faculty to accept and decide when my resignation will take effect.

In the Name of the Most Holy Trinity,

Rome, 15 February 1989, John Paul II PP.

Appendix 2

Excerpts from Pope John Paul II's Last Will and Testament, which was originally written in Polish, dated March 6, 1979, with successive additions:

The testament of 6.3.1979

In the Name of the Most Holy Trinity. Amen.

"Keep watch, because you do not know which day
when the Lord will come" (Matthew 4, 42) – These
words remind me of the final call, which will come the
moment that the Lord will choose. I desire to follow
Him and desire that all that is part of my earthly life
shall prepare me for this moment. I do not know
when it will come, but like all else, this moment, too, I
place into the hands of the Mother of my Master:
Totus Tuus. In the same maternal hands I place all
those with whom my life and vocation are bound. Into
these Hands I leave above all the Church, and also my
nation and all humanity. I thank everyone. To everyone I ask forgiveness. I also ask prayers, so that the
Mercy of God will grow greater than my weakness
and unworthiness.

I leave behind me some property which necessitates
disposal. Regarding those items of daily use of which I
made use, I ask that they be distributed as may appear
opportune. My personal notes are to be burned. I ask
that Don Stanislaw takes care of this and I thank him

for the collaboration and help so prolonged and so attentive over the years. All other thanks, instead, I leave in my heart before God Himself, because it is difficult to express them.

How many people should I list! Probably the Lord God has called to Himself the majority of them - as to those who are still on this side, may the words of this testament recall them, everyone and everywhere, wherever they are.

As the end of my life approaches I return with my memory to the beginning, to my parents, to my brother, to the sister (I never knew her because she died before my birth), to the parish in Wadowice, where I was baptized, to that city I love, to my contemporaries, my friends from school and university, up to the time of the Occupation when I was a worker, and then in the parish of Niegowic, then St Florian's in Krakow, to the pastoral ministry of academics, to Krakow and to Rome, to the people who were entrusted to me in a special way by the Lord.

To all I want to say just one thing: "May God reward you."

In manus tuas, Domine, commendo spiritum meum.
Into your hands, O Lord, I commend my spirit.

AD 17.III.2000